DICTIONARY
THEME–BASED

British English Collection

ENGLISH-
LITHUANIAN

The most useful words
To expand your lexicon and sharpen
your language skills

3000 words

Theme-based dictionary British English-Lithuanian - 3000 words
By Andrey Taranov

T&P Books vocabularies are intended for helping you learn, memorize and review foreign words. The dictionary is divided into themes, covering all major spheres of everyday activities, business, science, culture, etc.

The process of learning words using T&P Books' theme-based dictionaries gives you the following advantages:

- Correctly grouped source information predetermines success at subsequent stages of word memorization
- Availability of words derived from the same root allowing memorization of word units (rather than separate words)
- Small units of words facilitate the process of establishing associative links needed for consolidation of vocabulary
- Level of language knowledge can be estimated by the number of learned words

T&P Books Publishing
www.tpbooks.com

This book is also available in E-book formats.
Please visit www.tpbooks.com or the major online bookstores.

LITHUANIAN THEME-BASED DICTIONARY
British English collection

T&P Books vocabularies are intended to help you learn, memorize, and review foreign words. The vocabulary contains over 3000 commonly used words arranged thematically.

- Vocabulary contains the most commonly used words
- Recommended as an addition to any language course
- Meets the needs of beginners and advanced learners of foreign languages
- Convenient for daily use, revision sessions, and self-testing activities
- Allows you to assess your vocabulary

Special features of the vocabulary

- Words are organized according to their meaning, not alphabetically
- Words are presented in three columns to facilitate the reviewing and self-testing processes
- Words in groups are divided into small blocks to facilitate the learning process
- The vocabulary offers a convenient and simple transcription of each foreign word

The vocabulary has 101 topics including:

Basic Concepts, Numbers, Colors, Months, Seasons, Units of Measurement, Clothing & Accessories, Food & Nutrition, Restaurant, Family Members, Relatives, Character, Feelings, Emotions, Diseases, City, Town, Sightseeing, Shopping, Money, House, Home, Office, Working in the Office, Import & Export, Marketing, Job Search, Sports, Education, Computer, Internet, Tools, Nature, Countries, Nationalities and more ...

TABLE OF CONTENTS

PRONUNCIATION GUIDE

Letter	Lithuanian example	T&P phonetic alphabet	English example
Aa	adata	[a]	shorter than in 'ask'
Ąą	ąžuolas	[aː]	calf, palm
Bb	badas	[b]	baby, book
Cc	cukrus	[ts]	cats, tsetse fly
Čč	česnakas	[tʃ]	church, French
Dd	dumblas	[d]	day, doctor
Ee	eglė	[æ]	chess, man
Ęę	vedęs	[æː]	longer than in 'brand'
Ėė	ėdalas	[eː]	longer than in bell
Ff	fleita	[f]	face, food
Gg	gandras	[g]	game, gold
Hh	husaras	[ɣ]	between [g] and [h]
I i	ižas	[i]	shorter than in 'feet'
Į į	mįslė	[iː]	feet, meter
Yy	vynas	[iː]	feet, meter
J j	juokas	[j]	yes, New York
Kk	kilpa	[k]	clock, kiss
L l	laisvė	[l]	lace, people
Mm	mama	[m]	magic, milk
Nn	nauda	[n]	name, normal
Oo	ola	[o], [oː]	floor, doctor
Pp	pirtis	[p]	pencil, private
Rr	ragana	[r]	rice, radio
Ss	sostinė	[s]	city, boss
Šš	šūvis	[ʃ]	machine, shark
Tt	tėvynė	[t]	tourist, trip
Uu	upė	[u]	book
Ųų	siųsti	[uː]	pool, room
Ūū	ūmėdė	[uː]	pool, room
Vv	vabalas	[ʋ]	vase, winter
Zz	zuikis	[z]	zebra, please
Žž	žiurkė	[ʒ]	forge, pleasure

Comments

A macron (ū), an ogonek (ą, ę, į, ų) can all be used to mark vowel length in Modern Standard Lithuanian. Acute (Áá Ą́ą́), grave (Àà), and tilde (Ãã Ą̃ą̃) diacritics are used to indicate pitch accents. However, these pitch accents are generally not written, except in dictionaries, grammars, and where needed for clarity, such as to differentiate homonyms and dialectal use.

ABBREVIATIONS
used in the dictionary

English abbreviations

ab.	-	about
adj	-	adjective
adv	-	adverb
anim.	-	animate
as adj	-	attributive noun used as adjective
e.g.	-	for example
etc.	-	et cetera
fam.	-	familiar
fem.	-	feminine
form.	-	formal
inanim.	-	inanimate
masc.	-	masculine
math	-	mathematics
mil.	-	military
n	-	noun
pl	-	plural
pron.	-	pronoun
sb	-	somebody
sing.	-	singular
sth	-	something
v aux	-	auxiliary verb
vi	-	intransitive verb
vi, vt	-	intransitive, transitive verb
vt	-	transitive verb

Lithuanian abbreviations

dgs	-	plural
m	-	feminine noun
m dgs	-	feminine plural
v	-	masculine noun
v dgs	-	masculine plural

BASIC CONCEPTS

1. Pronouns

I, me	aš	['aʃ]
you	tu	['tu]
he	jis	[jɪs]
she	ji	[jɪ]
we	mēs	['mʲæs]
you (to a group)	jūs	['juːs]
they	jie	['jiɛ]

2. Greetings. Salutations

Hello! (fam.)	Sveikas!	['svʲɛɪkas!]
Hello! (form.)	Sveiki!	[svʲɛɪ'kʲɪ!]
Good morning!	Labas rýtas!	['lʲaːbas 'rʲiːtas!]
Good afternoon!	Labà dienà!	[lʲa'ba dʲɛ'na!]
Good evening!	Labas vãkaras!	['lʲaːbas 'vaːkaras!]

to say hello	sveikintis	['svʲɛɪkʲɪntʲɪs]
Hi! (hello)	Labas!	['lʲaːbas!]
greeting (n)	linkėjimas (v)	[lʲɪŋ'kʲɛjɪmas]
to greet (vt)	sveikinti	['svʲɛɪkʲɪntʲɪ]
How are you?	Kaip sėkasi?	['kʌɪp 'sʲækasʲɪ?]
What's new?	Kàs naūjo?	['kas 'nɑʊjɔ?]

Bye-Bye! Goodbye!	Iki pasimãtymo!	[ɪkʲɪ pasʲɪmatʲiːmo!]
See you soon!	Iki greĩto susìtikimo!	[ɪ'kʲɪ 'grʲɛɪtɔ susʲɪtʲɪ'kʲɪmɔ!]
Farewell!	Lìkite sveiki!	['lʲɪkʲɪtʲɛ svʲɛɪ'kʲɪ!]
to say goodbye	atsisveikinti	[atsʲɪ'svʲɛɪkʲɪntʲɪ]
Cheers!	Iki!	[ɪ'kʲɪ!]

Thank you! Cheers!	Ačiū!	['aːtʃʲuː!]
Thank you very much!	Labaĩ ačiū!	[lʲa'bʌɪ 'aːtʃʲuː!]
My pleasure!	Prašom.	['praːʃom]
Don't mention it!	Nevertà padėkõs.	[nʲɛver'ta padʲe:'ko:s]
It was nothing	Nėrà už ką̃.	[nʲeː'ra 'ʊʒ kaː]

Excuse me! (fam.)	Atléisk!	[at'lʲɛɪsk!]
Excuse me! (form.)	Atléiskite!	[at'lʲɛɪskʲɪtʲɛ!]
to excuse (forgive)	atléisti	[at'lʲɛɪstʲɪ]

to apologize (vi)	atsiprašýti	[atsʲɪpra'ʃɪːtʲɪ]
My apologies	Mãno atsiprãšymas.	['maːnɔ atsʲɪ'pra:ʃɪːmas]
I'm sorry!	Atléiskite!	[at'lʲɛɪskʲɪtʲɛ!]

to forgive (vt)	atleisti	[at'lʲɛɪstʲɪ]
It's okay! (that's all right)	Nieko baisaũs.	['nʲɛkɔ bʌɪ'sɑʊs]
please (adv)	prašom	['praːʃom]

Don't forget!	Nepamiřškite!	[nʲɛpa'mʲɪrʃkʲɪtʲɛ!]
Certainly!	Žinoma!	['ʒʲɪnoma!]
Of course not!	Žinoma nė!	['ʒʲɪnoma nʲɛ!]
Okay! (I agree)	Sutinku!	[sʊtʲɪŋ'kʊ!]
That's enough!	Užteks!	[ʊʒ'tʲɛks!]

3. Questions

Who?	Kas?	['kas?]
What?	Ką?	['kaː?]
Where? (at, in)	Kur?	['kʊr?]
Where (to)?	Kur?	['kʊr?]
From where?	Iš kur?	[ɪʃ 'kʊr?]
When?	Kada?	[ka'da?]
Why? (What for?)	Kam?	['kam?]
Why? (~ are you crying?)	Kodėl?	[kɔ'dʲeːlʲ?]

What for?	Kam?	['kam?]
How? (in what way)	Kaĩp?	['kʌɪp?]
What? (What kind of ...?)	Koks?	['koks?]
Which?	Kuris?	[kʊ'rʲɪs?]

To whom?	Kam?	['kam?]
About whom?	Apiė ką?	[a'pʲɛ 'kaː?]
About what?	Apiė ką?	[a'pʲɛ 'kaː?]
With whom?	Sù kuõ?	['sʊ 'kʊɑ?]

| How many? How much? | Kiek? | ['kʲiɛk?] |
| Whose? | Kieno? | [kʲiɛ'noː?] |

4. Prepositions

with (accompanied by)	sù ...	['sʊ ...]
without	bė	['bʲɛ]
to (indicating direction)	į	[iː]
about (talking ~ ...)	apiė	[a'pʲɛ]
before (in time)	iki	[ɪ'kʲɪ]
in front of ...	priẽš	['prʲɛʃ]

under (beneath, below)	põ	['poː]
above (over)	viřš	['vʲɪrʃ]
on (atop)	ant	['ant]

| from (off, out of) | iš | [ɪʃ] |
| of (made from) | iš | [ɪʃ] |

| in (e.g. ~ ten minutes) | põ ..., ùž ... | ['poː: ...], ['ʊʒ ...] |
| over (across the top of) | per | ['pʲɛr] |

5. Function words. Adverbs. Part 1

Where? (at, in)	Kur?	['kʊr?]
here (adv)	čia	['tsʲæ]
there (adv)	ten	['tʲɛn]
somewhere (to be)	kažkur	[kaʒ'kʊr]
nowhere (not in any place)	niekur	['nʲɛkʊr]
by (near, beside)	prie …	['prʲɛ …]
by the window	prie lango	['prʲɛ 'lʲangɔ]
Where (to)?	Kur?	['kʊr?]
here (e.g. come ~!)	čia	['tsʲæ]
there (e.g. to go ~)	ten	['tʲɛn]
from here (adv)	iš čia	[ɪʃ tsʲæ]
from there (adv)	iš ten	[ɪʃ tʲɛn]
close (adv)	šalia	[ʃa'lʲæ]
far (adv)	toli	[to'lʲɪ]
near (e.g. ~ Paris)	šalia	[ʃa'lʲæ]
nearby (adv)	arti	[ar'tʲɪ]
not far (adv)	netoli	[nʲɛ'tolʲɪ]
left (adj)	kairys	[kʌɪ'rʲi:s]
on the left	iš kairės	[ɪʃ kʌɪ'rʲe:s]
to the left	į kairę	[i: 'kʌɪrʲɛ:]
right (adj)	dešinys	[dʲɛʃɪ'nʲi:s]
on the right	iš dešinės	[ɪʃ deʃɪ'nʲe:s]
to the right	į dešinę	[i: 'dʲæʃɪnʲɛ:]
in front (adv)	priekyje	['prʲɛkʲi:jɛ]
front (as adj)	priekinis	['prʲɛkʲɪnʲɪs]
ahead (the kids ran ~)	pirmyn	[pʲɪr'mʲi:n]
behind (adv)	gale	[ga'lʲɛ]
from behind	iš galo	[ɪʃ 'ga:lʲɔ]
back (towards the rear)	atgal	[at'galʲ]
middle	vidurys (v)	[vʲɪdu'rʲi:s]
in the middle	per vidurį	['pʲɛr 'vʲɪːdʊrʲɪ:]
at the side	šone	['ʃonʲɛ]
everywhere (adv)	visur	[vʲɪ'sʊr]
around (in all directions)	aplinkui	[ap'lʲɪŋkʊi]
from inside	iš vidaus	[ɪʃ vʲɪ'daʊs]
somewhere (to go)	kažkur	[kaʒ'kʊr]
straight (directly)	tiesiai	['tʲɛsʲɛɪ]
back (e.g. come ~)	atgal	[at'galʲ]
from anywhere	iš kur nors	[ɪʃ 'kʊr 'nors]
from somewhere	iš kažkur	[ɪʃ kaʒ'kʊr]

13

firstly (adv)	pìrma	['pʲɪrma]
secondly (adv)	àntra	['antra]
thirdly (adv)	trẽčia	['trʲætʃʲæ]

suddenly (adv)	staigà	[stʌɪ'ga]
at first (in the beginning)	pradžiõj	[prad'ʒʲoːj]
for the first time	pìrmą kãrtą	['pʲɪrma: 'karta:]
long before ...	daũg laĩko priẽš ...	['daʊg 'lʲʌɪkɔ 'prʲɛʃ ...]
anew (over again)	ìš naũjo	[ɪʃ 'nɔʊjɔ]
for good (adv)	visám laĩkui	[vʲɪ'sam 'lʲʌɪkʊi]

never (adv)	niekadà	[nʲiɛkad'a]
again (adv)	vėl	['vʲeːlʲ]
now (at present)	dabar̃	[da'bar]
often (adv)	dažnaĩ	[daʒ'nʌɪ]
then (adv)	tadà	[ta'da]
urgently (quickly)	skubiaĩ	[skʊ'bʲɛɪ]
usually (adv)	įprastaĩ	[iːpras'tʌɪ]

by the way, ...	bejè, ...	[bɛ'jæ, ...]
possibly	įmãnoma	[iː'maːnoma]
probably (adv)	tikėtina	[tɪr'kʲeːtʲɪna]
maybe (adv)	gãli bū́ti	['gaːlʲɪ 'buːtʲɪ]
besides ...	bè tõ, ...	['bʲɛ to:, ...]
that's why ...	todėl ...	[to'dʲeːlʲ ...]
in spite of ...	nepáisant ...	[nʲɛ'pʌɪsant ...]
thanks to ...	... dėkà	[... dʲe:'ka]

what (pron.)	kàs	['kas]
that (conj.)	kàs	['kas]
something	kažkàs	[kaʒ'kas]
anything (something)	kažkàs	[kaʒ'kas]
nothing	niẽko	['nʲɛkɔ]

who (pron.)	kàs	['kas]
someone	kažkàs	[kaʒ'kas]
somebody	kažkàs	[kaʒ'kas]

nobody	niẽkas	['nʲɛkas]
nowhere (a voyage to ~)	niẽkur	['nʲɛkʊr]
nobody's	niẽkieno	['nʲɛ'kʲiɛnɔ]
somebody's	kažkienõ	[kaʒkʲiɛ'no:]

so (I'm ~ glad)	taĩp	['tʌɪp]
also (as well)	taĩp pàt	['tʌɪp 'pat]
too (as well)	ír̃gi	['ɪrgʲɪ]

6. Function words. Adverbs. Part 2

Why?	Kodėl?	[kɔ'dʲeːlʲʔ]
for some reason	kažkodėl	[kaʒko'dʲeːlʲ]
because ...	... todėl, kàd	[... to'dʲeːlʲ, 'kad]
for some purpose	kažkodėl	[kaʒko'dʲeːlʲ]
and	ír̃	[ɪr]

or	**arbà**	[ar'ba]
but	**bèt**	['bʲɛt]
too (excessively)	**pernelýg**	[pʲɛrnʲɛ'lʲi:g]
only (exclusively)	**tiktaĩ**	[tʲɪk'tʌɪ]
exactly (adv)	**tiksliaĩ**	[tʲɪks'lʲɛɪ]
about (more or less)	**maždaũg**	[maʒ'dɑʊg]
approximately (adv)	**apýtikriai**	[a'pʲi:tʲɪkrʲɛɪ]
approximate (adj)	**apýtikriai**	[a'pʲi:tʲɪkrʲɛɪ]
almost (adv)	**bevéik**	[bʲɛ'vʲɛɪk]
the rest	**vìsa kìta** (m)	['vʲɪsa 'kʲɪta]
each (adj)	**kiekvíenas**	[kʲiɛk'vʲiɛnas]
any (no matter which)	**bèt kurìs**	['bʲɛt kʊ'rʲɪs]
many, much (a lot of)	**daũg**	['dɑʊg]
many people	**daũgelis**	['dɑʊgʲɛlʲɪs]
all (everyone)	**visì**	[vʲɪ'sʲɪ]
in return for ...	**mainaĩs į̃ ...**	[mʌɪ'nʌɪs i: ..]
in exchange (adv)	**mainaĩs**	[mʌɪ'nʌɪs]
by hand (made)	**rañkiniu būdù**	['raŋkʲɪnʲʊ bu:'dʊ]
hardly (negative opinion)	**kažì**	[ka'ʒʲɪ]
probably (adv)	**tikriáusiai**	[tʲɪk'rʲæʊsʲɛɪ]
on purpose (intentionally)	**týčia**	['tʲi:tʂʲæ]
by accident (adv)	**netýčia**	[nʲɛ'tʲi:tʂʲæ]
very (adv)	**labaĩ**	[lʲa'bʌɪ]
for example (adv)	**pãvyzdžiui**	['pa:vʲi:zdʒʲʊi]
between	**tar̃p**	['tarp]
among	**tar̃p**	['tarp]
so much (such a lot)	**tiẽk**	['tʲɛk]
especially (adv)	**ýpač**	['ɪ:patʂ]

NUMBERS. MISCELLANEOUS

7. Cardinal numbers. Part 1

0 zero	nulis	['nʊlʲɪs]
1 one	vienas	['vʲiɛnas]
2 two	du	['dʊ]
3 three	tris	['trʲɪs]
4 four	keturi	[kʲɛtʊ'rʲɪ]
5 five	penki	[pʲɛŋ'kʲɪ]
6 six	šeši	[ʃɛ'ʃɪ]
7 seven	septyni	[sʲɛptʲiː'nʲɪ]
8 eight	aštuoni	[aʃtʊɑ'nʲɪ]
9 nine	devyni	[dʲɛvʲiː'nʲɪ]
10 ten	dešimt	['dʲæʃɪmt]
11 eleven	vienuolika	[vʲiɛ'nʊɑlʲɪka]
12 twelve	dvylika	['dvʲiːlʲɪka]
13 thirteen	trylika	['trʲiːlʲɪka]
14 fourteen	keturiolika	[kʲɛtʊ'rʲɪolʲɪka]
15 fifteen	penkiolika	[pʲɛŋ'kʲolʲɪka]
16 sixteen	šešiolika	[ʃɛ'ʃolʲɪka]
17 seventeen	septyniolika	[sʲɛptʲiː'nʲɪolʲɪka]
18 eighteen	aštuoniolika	[aʃtʊɑ'nʲɪolʲɪka]
19 nineteen	devyniolika	[dʲɛvʲiː'nʲɪolʲɪka]
20 twenty	dvidešimt	['dvʲɪdʲɛʃɪmt]
21 twenty-one	dvidešimt vienas	['dvʲɪdʲɛʃɪmt 'vʲiɛnas]
22 twenty-two	dvidešimt du	['dvʲɪdʲɛʃɪmt 'dʊ]
23 twenty-three	dvidešimt tris	['dvʲɪdʲɛʃɪmt 'trʲɪs]
30 thirty	trisdešimt	['trʲɪsdʲɛʃɪmt]
31 thirty-one	trisdešimt vienas	['trʲɪsdʲɛʃɪmt 'vʲiɛnas]
32 thirty-two	trisdešimt du	['trʲɪsdʲɛʃɪmt 'dʊ]
33 thirty-three	trisdešimt tris	['trʲɪsdʲɛʃɪmt 'trʲɪs]
40 forty	keturiasdešimt	['kʲætʊrʲæsdʲɛʃɪmt]
41 forty-one	keturiasdešimt vienas	['kʲætʊrʲæsdʲɛʃɪmt 'vʲiɛnas]
42 forty-two	keturiasdešimt du	['kʲætʊrʲæsdʲɛʃɪmt 'dʊ]
43 forty-three	keturiasdešimt tris	['kʲætʊrʲæsdʲɛʃɪmt 'trʲɪs]
50 fifty	penkiasdešimt	['pʲɛŋkʲæsdʲɛʃɪmt]
51 fifty-one	penkiasdešimt vienas	['pʲɛŋkʲæsdʲɛʃɪmt 'vʲiɛnas]
52 fifty-two	penkiasdešimt du	['pʲɛŋkʲæsdʲɛʃɪmt 'dʊ]
53 fifty-three	penkiasdešimt tris	['pʲɛŋkʲæsdʲɛʃɪmt 'trʲɪs]
60 sixty	šešiasdešimt	['ʃæʃæsdʲɛʃɪmt]
61 sixty-one	šešiasdešimt vienas	['ʃæʃæsdʲɛʃɪmt 'vʲiɛnas]

| 62 sixty-two | šešiasdešimt dù | ['ʃæʃæsdˈɛʃɪmt 'dʊ] |
| 63 sixty-three | šešiasdešimt trìs | ['ʃæʃæsdˈɛʃɪmt 'trˈɪs] |

70 seventy	septyniasdešimt	[sˈɛpˈtˈiːnˈæsdˈɛʃɪmt]
71 seventy-one	septyniasdešimt víenas	[sˈɛpˈtˈiːnˈæsdˈɛʃɪmt 'vˈiɛnas]
72 seventy-two	septyniasdešimt dù	[sˈɛpˈtˈiːnˈæsdˈɛʃɪmt 'dʊ]
73 seventy-three	septyniasdešimt trìs	[sˈɛptˈiːnˈæsdˈɛʃɪmt 'trˈɪs]

80 eighty	aštuoniasdešimt	[aʃˈtʊɑnˈæsdˈɛʃɪmt]
81 eighty-one	aštúoniasdešimt víenas	[aʃˈtʊɑnˈæsdˈɛʃɪmt 'vˈiɛnas]
82 eighty-two	aštúoniasdešimt dù	[aʃˈtʊɑnˈæsdˈɛʃɪmt 'dʊ]
83 eighty-three	aštúoniasdešimt trìs	[aʃˈtʊɑnˈæsdˈɛʃɪmt 'trˈɪs]

90 ninety	devyniasdešimt	[dˈɛ'vˈiːnˈæsdˈɛʃɪmt]
91 ninety-one	devyniasdešimt víenas	[dˈɛ'vˈiːnˈæsdˈɛʃɪmt 'vˈiɛnas]
92 ninety-two	devyniasdešimt dù	[dˈɛ'vˈiːnˈæsdˈɛʃɪmt 'dʊ]
93 ninety-three	devyniasdešimt trìs	[dˈɛ'vˈiːnˈæsdˈɛʃɪmt 'trˈɪs]

8. Cardinal numbers. Part 2

100 one hundred	šimtas	['ʃɪmtas]
200 two hundred	dù šimtaì	['dʊ ʃɪm'tʌɪ]
300 three hundred	trìs šimtaì	['trˈɪs ʃɪm'tʌɪ]
400 four hundred	keturì šimtaì	[kˈɛtʊ'rˈɪ ʃɪm'tʌɪ]
500 five hundred	penkì šimtaì	[pˈɛŋ'kˈɪ ʃɪm'tʌɪ]

600 six hundred	šešì šimtaì	[ʃɛ'ʃˈɪ ʃɪm'tʌɪ]
700 seven hundred	septynì šimtaì	[sˈɛptˈiːn'ɪ 'ʃɪmtʌɪ]
800 eight hundred	aštuonì šimtaì	[aʃtʊɑ'nˈɪ ʃɪm'tʌɪ]
900 nine hundred	devynì šimtaì	[dˈɛvˈiː'nˈɪ ʃɪm'tʌɪ]

1000 one thousand	tū̃kstantis	['tuːkstantˈɪs]
2000 two thousand	dù tū̃kstančiai	['dʊ 'tuːkstantʂˈɛɪ]
3000 three thousand	trỹs tū̃kstančiai	['trˈiːs 'tuːkstantʂˈɛɪ]
10000 ten thousand	dẽšimt tū̃kstančių	['dˈæʃɪmt 'tuːkstantʂˈuː]
one hundred thousand	šìmtas tū̃kstančių	['ʃɪmtas 'tuːkstantʂˈuː]
million	milijõnas (v)	[mˈɪlˈɪ'joːnas]
billion	milijárdas (v)	[mˈɪlˈɪ'jardas]

9. Ordinal numbers

first (adj)	pìrmas	['pˈɪrmas]
second (adj)	añtras	['antras]
third (adj)	trẽčias	['trˈætʂˈæs]
fourth (adj)	ketvìrtas	[kˈɛt'vˈɪrtas]
fifth (adj)	peñktas	['pˈɛŋktas]

sixth (adj)	šẽštas	['ʃæʃtas]
seventh (adj)	septiñtas	[sˈɛp'tˈɪntas]
eighth (adj)	aštuñtas	[aʃˈtʊntas]
ninth (adj)	deviñtas	[dˈɛ'vˈɪntas]
tenth (adj)	dešimtas	[dˈɛ'ʃɪmtas]

COLORS. UNITS OF MEASUREMENT

10. Colours

colour	spalva (m)	[spalʲ'va]
shade (tint)	ãtspalvis (v)	['a:tspalʲvʲɪs]
hue	tònas (v)	['tonas]
rainbow	vaivórykštė (m)	[vʌɪ'vorʲi:kʃtʲe:]

white (adj)	balta	[balʲ'ta]
black (adj)	juoda	[juɑ'da]
grey (adj)	pilka	[pʲɪlʲ'ka]

green (adj)	žalia	[ʒa'lʲiæ]
yellow (adj)	geltóna	[gʲɛlʲ'tona]
red (adj)	raudóna	[rɑu'dona]

blue (adj)	mėlyna	['mʲe:lʲi:na]
light blue (adj)	žydra	[ʒʲi:d'ra]
pink (adj)	rožinė	['ro:ʒʲɪnʲe:]
orange (adj)	oránžinė	[o'ranʒʲɪnʲe:]
violet (adj)	violetinė	[vʲɪjo'lʲɛtʲɪnʲe:]
brown (adj)	ruda	[ru'da]

golden (adj)	auksìnis	[ɑuk'sʲɪnʲɪs]
silvery (adj)	sidabrìnis	[sʲɪda'brʲɪnʲɪs]

beige (adj)	smėlio spalvõs	['smʲe:lʲɔ spalʲ'vo:s]
cream (adj)	kreminės spalvõs	['krʲɛmʲɪnʲe:s spalʲ'vo:s]
turquoise (adj)	turkio spalvõs	['turkʲɔ spalʲ'vo:s]
cherry red (adj)	vyšnių spalvõs	[vʲi:ʃnʲu: spalʲ'vo:s]
lilac (adj)	alyvų spalvõs	[a'lʲi:vu: spalʲ'vo:s]
crimson (adj)	avietinės spalvõs	[a'vʲɛtʲɪnʲe:s spalʲ'vo:s]

light (adj)	šviesì	[ʃvʲiɛ'sʲɪ]
dark (adj)	tamsì	[tam'sʲɪ]
bright, vivid (adj)	ryškì	[rʲi:ʃkʲɪ]

coloured (pencils)	spalvótas	[spalʲ'votas]
colour (e.g. ~ film)	spalvótas	[spalʲ'votas]
black-and-white (adj)	juodaì báltas	[juɑ'dʌɪ 'balʲtas]
plain (one-coloured)	vienspálvis	[vʲiɛns'palʲvʲɪs]
multicoloured (adj)	įvairiaspálvis	[i:vʌɪrʲæs'palʲvʲɪs]

11. Units of measurement

weight	svõris (v)	['svo:rʲɪs]
length	ìlgis (v)	[iʲlgʲɪs]

width	plótis (v)	['pl'oːt'ɪs]
height	aúkštis (v)	['ɑʊkʃt'ɪs]
depth	gýlis (v)	['g'iːl'ɪs]
volume	tūris (v)	['tuːr'ɪs]
area	plótas (v)	['pl'otas]

gram	grãmas (v)	['graːmas]
milligram	miligrãmas (v)	[m'ɪl'ɪ'graːmas]
kilogram	kilogrãmas (v)	[k'ɪl'o'graːmas]
ton	tonà (m)	[to'na]
pound	svãras (v)	['svaːras]
ounce	ùncija (m)	['ʊnts'ɪjɛ]

metre	mètras (v)	['m'ɛtras]
millimetre	milimètras (v)	[m'ɪl'ɪ'm'ɛtras]
centimetre	centimètras (v)	[ts'ɛnt'ɪ'm'ɛtras]
kilometre	kilomètras (v)	[k'ɪl'o'm'ɛtras]
mile	mylià (m)	[m'iːl'æ]

inch	cólis (v)	['tsol'ɪs]
foot	pėdà (m)	[p'eː'da]
yard	jãrdas (v)	[jardas]

square metre	kvadrãtinis mètras (v)	[kvad'raːt'ɪn'ɪs 'm'ɛtras]
hectare	hektãras (v)	[ɣ'ɛk'taːras]

litre	lìtras (v)	['l'ɪtras]
degree	laĩpsnis (v)	['l'ʌɪpsn'ɪs]
volt	vòltas (v)	['vol'tas]
ampere	ampèras (v)	[am'p'ɛras]
horsepower	ãrklio galià (m)	['arkl'ɔ ga'l'æ]

quantity	kiẽkis (v)	['k'ɛk'ɪs]
a little bit of ...	nedaũg ...	[n'ɛ'dɑʊg ...]
half	pùsė (m)	['pʊs'eː]
dozen	tùzinas (v)	['tʊz'ɪnas]
piece (item)	víenetas (v)	['v'ɪɛn'ɛtas]

size	dýdis (v), išmatãvimai (v dgs)	['d'iːd'ɪs], [iʃma'taːv'ɪmʌɪ]
scale (map ~)	mastèlis (v)	[mas't'æl'ɪs]

minimal (adj)	minimalùs	[m'ɪn'ɪma'l'ʊs]
the smallest (adj)	mažiáusias	[ma'ʒ'æʊs'æs]
medium (adj)	vidutìnis	[v'ɪdʊ't'ɪn'ɪs]
maximal (adj)	maksimalùs	[maks'ɪma'l'ʊs]
the largest (adj)	didžiáusias	[d'ɪ'dʒ'æʊs'æs]

12. Containers

canning jar (glass ~)	stiklaĩnis (v)	[st'ɪk'l'ʌɪn'ɪs]
tin, can	skardìnė (m)	[skar'd'ɪn'eː]
bucket	kìbiras (v)	['k'ɪb'ɪras]
barrel	statìnė (m)	[sta't'ɪn'e:]
wash basin (e.g., plastic ~)	dubenėlis (v)	[dʊbe'n'eːl'ɪs]

tank (100L water ~)	bãkas (v)	['ba:kas]
hip flask	kolba (m)	['kolʲba]
jerrycan	kanìstras (v)	[ka'nʲɪstras]
tank (e.g., tank car)	bãkas (v)	['ba:kas]
mug	puodẽlis (v)	[pʊɑ'dʲælʲɪs]
cup (of coffee, etc.)	puodẽlis (v)	[pʊɑ'dʲælʲɪs]
saucer	lẽkštẽlẽ (m)	[lʲe:kʃ'tʲælʲe:]
glass (tumbler)	stìklas (v)	['stʲɪklʲas]
wine glass	taurẽ (m)	[tɑʊ'rʲe:]
stock pot (soup pot)	púodas (v)	['pʊɑdas]
bottle (~ of wine)	bùtelis (v)	['bʊtʲɛlʲɪs]
neck (of the bottle, etc.)	kãklas (v)	['ka:klʲas]
carafe (decanter)	grafìnas (v)	[gra'fʲɪnas]
pitcher	ąsõtis (v)	[a:'so:tʲɪs]
vessel (container)	ìndas (v)	['ɪndas]
pot (crock, stoneware ~)	púodas (v)	['pʊɑdas]
vase	vazà (m)	[va'za]
flacon, bottle (perfume ~)	bùtelis (v)	['bʊtʲɛlʲɪs]
vial, small bottle	buteliùkas (v)	[bʊtʲɛ'lʲʊkas]
tube (of toothpaste)	tūbà (m)	[tu:'ba]
sack (bag)	maĩšas (v)	['mʌɪʃas]
bag (paper ~, plastic ~)	pakètas (v)	[pa'kʲɛtas]
packet (of cigarettes, etc.)	plúoštas (v)	['plʲʊɑʃtas]
box (e.g. shoebox)	dẽžẽ (m)	[dʲe:'ʒʲe:]
crate	dẽžẽ (m)	[dʲe:'ʒʲe:]
basket	krepšỹs (v)	[krʲɛp'ʃʲɪ:s]

MAIN VERBS

to advise (vt)	patarinéti	[patar'ı'nʲe:tʲɪ]
to agree (say yes)	sutìkti	[sʊ'tʲɪktʲɪ]
to answer (vi, vt)	atsakýti	[atsa'kʲi:tʲɪ]
to apologize (vi)	atsiprašinéti	[atsʲɪpraʃʲɪ'nʲe:tʲɪ]
to arrive (vi)	atvažiúoti	[atva'ʒʲʊatʲɪ]

to ask (~ oneself)	kláusti	['klʲaʊstʲɪ]
to ask (~ sb to do sth)	prašýti	[pra'ʃɪ:tʲɪ]
to be (vi)	búti	['bu:tʲɪ]

to be afraid	bijóti	[bʲɪ'jɔtʲɪ]
to be hungry	noréti válgyti	[no'rʲe:tʲɪ 'valʲgʲi:tʲɪ]
to be interested in ...	dométis	[do'mʲe:tʲɪs]
to be needed	búti reikalìngu	['bu:tʲɪ rʲɛɪka'lʲɪngʊ]
to be surprised	stebétis	[ste'bʲe:tʲɪs]
to be thirsty	noréti gérti	[no'rʲe:tʲɪ 'gʲærtʲɪ]
to begin (vt)	pradéti	[pra'dʲe:tʲɪ]
to belong to ...	priklausýti	[prʲɪklʲaʊ'sʲi:tʲɪ]
to boast (vi)	gìrtis	['gʲɪrtʲɪs]
to break (split into pieces)	láužyti	['lʲaʊʒʲi:tʲɪ]
to call (~ for help)	kviẽsti	['kvʲɛstʲɪ]

can (v aux)	galéti	[ga'lʲe:tʲɪ]
to catch (vt)	gáudyti	['gaʊdʲi:tʲɪ]
to change (vt)	pakeìsti	[pa'kʲɛɪstʲɪ]
to choose (select)	išsirìnkti	[ɪʃsʲɪ'rʲɪŋktʲɪ]
to come down (the stairs)	leìstis	['lʲɛɪstʲɪs]
to compare (vt)	lýginti	['lʲi:gʲɪntʲɪ]
to complain (vi, vt)	skųstis	['sku:stʲɪs]
to confuse (mix up)	suklýsti	[sʊk'lʲi:stʲɪ]
to continue (vt)	tęsti	['tʲɛ:stʲɪ]
to control (vt)	kontroliúoti	[kontro'lʲʊatʲɪ]
to cook (dinner)	gamìnti	[ga'mʲɪntʲɪ]

to cost (vt)	kainúoti	[kʌɪ'nʊatʲɪ]
to count (add up)	skaičiúoti	[skʌɪ'tʂʲʊatʲɪ]
to count on ...	tikétis ...	[tʲɪ'kʲe:tʲɪs ...]
to create (vt)	sukùrti	[sʊ'kʊrtʲɪ]
to cry (weep)	ver̃kti	['vʲɛrktʲɪ]

to deceive (vi, vt)	apgaudinéti	[apgaʊdʲɪ'nʲe:tʲɪ]
to decorate (tree, street)	puõšti	['pʊaʃtʲɪ]

to defend (a country, etc.)	giñti	['gⁱɪntⁱɪ]
to demand (request firmly)	reikaláuti	[rⁱɛɪka'lⁱɑʊtⁱɪ]
to dig (vt)	raũsti	['rɑʊstⁱɪ]
to discuss (vt)	aptarinéti	[aptarⁱɪ'nⁱætⁱɪ]
to do (vt)	darýti	[da'rⁱi:tⁱɪ]
to doubt (have doubts)	abejóti	[abⁱɛ'jɔtⁱɪ]
to drop (let fall)	numèsti	[nʊ'mⁱɛstⁱɪ]
to enter (room, house, etc.)	įeĩti	[i:'ɛɪtⁱɪ]
to excuse (forgive)	atléisti	[at'lⁱɛɪstⁱɪ]
to exist (vi)	egzistúoti	[ɛgzⁱɪs'tʊɑtⁱɪ]
to expect (foresee)	numatýti	[nʊma'tⁱi:tⁱɪ]
to explain (vt)	paáiškinti	[pa'ʌɪʃkⁱɪntⁱɪ]
to fall (vi)	krìsti	['krⁱɪstⁱɪ]
to fancy (vt)	patìkti	[pa'tⁱɪktⁱɪ]
to find (vt)	ràsti	['rastⁱɪ]
to finish (vt)	užbaĩgti	[ʊʒ'bʌɪktⁱɪ]
to fly (vi)	skrìsti	['skrⁱɪstⁱɪ]
to follow … (come after)	sèkti …	['sⁱɛktⁱɪ …]
to forget (vi, vt)	užmìršti	[ʊʒ'mⁱɪrʃtⁱɪ]
to forgive (vt)	atléisti	[at'lⁱɛɪstⁱɪ]
to give (vt)	dúoti	['dʊɑtⁱɪ]
to give a hint	užsimiñti	[ʊʒsⁱɪ'mⁱɪntⁱɪ]
to go (on foot)	eĩti	['ɛɪtⁱɪ]
to go for a swim	máudytis	['mɑʊdⁱi:tⁱɪs]
to go out (for dinner, etc.)	išeĩti	[ɪ'ʃɛɪtⁱɪ]
to guess (the answer)	atspéti	[at'spⁱe:tⁱɪ]
to have (vt)	turéti	[tʊ'rⁱe:tⁱɪ]
to have breakfast	pusryčiauti	['pʊsrⁱi:tʃⁱɛʊtⁱɪ]
to have dinner	vakarieniáuti	[vakarⁱiɛ'nⁱæʊtⁱɪ]
to have lunch	pietáuti	[pⁱiɛ'tɑʊtⁱɪ]
to hear (vt)	girdéti	[gⁱɪr'dⁱe:tⁱɪ]
to help (vt)	padéti	[pa'dⁱe:tⁱɪ]
to hide (vt)	slḗpti	['slⁱe:ptⁱɪ]
to hope (vi, vt)	tikétis	[tⁱɪ'kⁱe:tⁱɪs]
to hunt (vi, vt)	medžióti	[mⁱɛ'dʒⁱɔtⁱɪ]
to hurry (vi)	skubéti	[skʊ'bⁱe:tⁱɪ]

15. The most important verbs. Part 3

to inform (vt)	informúoti	[ɪnfor'mʊɑtⁱɪ]
to insist (vi, vt)	reikaláuti	[rⁱɛɪka'lⁱɑʊtⁱɪ]
to insult (vt)	įžeidinéti	[i:ʒⁱɛɪdⁱɪ'nⁱe:tⁱɪ]
to invite (vt)	kviẽsti	['kvⁱɛstⁱɪ]
to joke (vi)	juokáuti	[jʊɑ'kɑʊtⁱɪ]
to keep (vt)	sáugoti	['sɑʊgotⁱɪ]
to keep silent, to hush	tyléti	[tⁱi:'lⁱe:tⁱɪ]

to kill (vt)	žudýti	[ʒʊ'dʲiːtʲɪ]
to know (sb)	pažinóti	[paʒʲɪ'notʲɪ]
to know (sth)	žinóti	[ʒʲɪ'notʲɪ]
to laugh (vi)	juóktis	['jʊaktʲɪs]

to liberate (city, etc.)	išláisvinti	[ɪʃʲlʲʌɪsvʲɪntʲɪ]
to look for ... (search)	ieškóti	[ɪɛʃʲkotʲɪ]
to love (sb)	myléti	[mʲiː'lʲeːtʲɪ]
to make a mistake	klýsti	['klʲiːstʲɪ]
to manage, to run	vadováuti	[vado'vaʊtʲɪ]

to mean (signify)	réikšti	['rʲɛɪkʃtʲɪ]
to mention (talk about)	minéti	[mʲɪ'nʲeːtʲɪ]
to miss (school, etc.)	praleidinéti	[pralʲɛɪdʲɪ'rʲnʲeːtʲɪ]
to notice (see)	pastebéti	[paste'bʲeːtʲɪ]
to object (vi, vt)	prieštaráuti	[prʲiɛʃta'raʊtʲɪ]

to observe (see)	stebéti	[ste'bʲeːtʲɪ]
to open (vt)	atidarýti	[atʲɪda'rʲiːtʲɪ]
to order (meal, etc.)	užsakinéti	[ʊʒsakʲɪ'nʲeːtʲɪ]
to order (mil.)	nurodinéti	[nʊrodʲɪ'nʲeːtʲɪ]
to own (possess)	mokéti	[mo'kʲeːtʲɪ]

to participate (vi)	dalyváuti	[dalʲiː'vaʊtʲɪ]
to pay (vi, vt)	mokéti	[mo'kʲeːtʲɪ]
to permit (vt)	léisti	['lʲɛɪstʲɪ]
to plan (vt)	planúoti	[plʲa'nʊatʲɪ]
to play (children)	žáisti	['ʒʌɪstʲɪ]

to pray (vi, vt)	mélstis	['mʲɛlʲstʲɪs]
to prefer (vt)	téikti pirmenýbę	['tʲɛɪktʲɪ pʲɪrmʲɛ'nʲiːbʲɛː]
to promise (vt)	žadéti	[ʒa'dʲeːtʲɪ]
to pronounce (vt)	ištárti	[ɪʃ'tartʲɪ]
to propose (vt)	siúlyti	['sʲuːlʲiːtʲɪ]
to punish (vt)	baústi	['baʊstʲɪ]

16. The most important verbs. Part 4

to read (vi, vt)	skaitýti	[skʌɪ'tʲiːtʲɪ]
to recommend (vt)	rekomendúoti	[rʲɛkomʲɛn'dʊatʲɪ]
to refuse (vi, vt)	atsisakýti	[atsʲɪsa'kʲiːtʲɪ]
to regret (be sorry)	gailétis	[gʌɪ'lʲeːtʲɪs]
to rent (sth from sb)	núomotis	['nʊamotʲɪs]

to repeat (say again)	kartóti	[kar'totʲɪ]
to reserve, to book	rezervúoti	[rʲɛzʲɛr'vʊatʲɪ]
to run (vi)	bégti	['bʲeːktʲɪ]
to save (rescue)	gélbéti	['gʲælʲbʲeːtʲɪ]

to say (~ thank you)	pasakýti	[pasa'kʲiːtʲɪ]
to scold (vt)	bárti	['bartʲɪ]
to see (vt)	matýti	[ma'tʲiːtʲɪ]
to sell (vt)	pardavinéti	[pardavʲɪ'nʲeːtʲɪ]
to send (vt)	išsiųsti	[ɪʃ'sʲuːstʲɪ]

to shoot (vi)	šaudyti	[ˈʃɑʊdʲiːtʲɪ]
to shout (vi)	šaūkti	[ˈʃɑʊktʲɪ]
to show (vt)	rodyti	[ˈrodʲiːtʲɪ]
to sign (document)	pasirašinéti	[pasʲɪraʃɪˈnʲeːtʲɪ]

to sit down (vi)	séstis	[ˈsʲeːstʲɪs]
to smile (vi)	šypsótis	[ʃɪːpˈsotʲɪs]
to speak (vi, vt)	sakýti	[saˈkʲiːtʲɪ]
to steal (money, etc.)	võgti	[ˈvoːktʲɪ]
to stop (for pause, etc.)	sustóti	[sʊsˈtotʲɪ]

to stop (please ~ calling me)	nustóti	[nʊˈstotʲɪ]
to study (vt)	studijúoti	[stʊdʲɪˈjʊatʲɪ]
to swim (vi)	plaūkti	[ˈplʲɑʊktʲɪ]
to take (vt)	imti	[ˈɪmtʲɪ]
to think (vi, vt)	galvóti	[galʲˈvotʲɪ]

to threaten (vt)	grasìnti	[graˈsʲɪntʲɪ]
to touch (with hands)	čiupinéti	[tʃʲʊpʲɪˈnʲeːtʲɪ]
to translate (vt)	veřsti	[ˈvʲɛrstʲɪ]
to trust (vt)	pasitikéti	[pasʲɪtʲɪˈkʲeːtʲɪ]
to try (attempt)	bandýti	[banˈdʲiːtʲɪ]

to turn (e.g., ~ left)	sùkti	[ˈsʊktʲɪ]
to underestimate (vt)	nejvértinti	[nʲɛɪˈvʲɛrtʲɪntʲɪ]
to understand (vt)	supràsti	[sʊpˈrastʲɪ]
to unite (vt)	apjùngti	[aˈpjʊŋktʲɪ]
to wait (vt)	laukti	[ˈlʲɑʊktʲɪ]

to want (wish, desire)	noréti	[noˈrʲeːtʲɪ]
to warn (vt)	pérspéti	[ˈpʲɛrspʲeːtʲɪ]
to work (vi)	dìrbti	[ˈdʲɪrptʲɪ]
to write (vt)	rašýti	[raˈʃɪːtʲɪ]
to write down	užrašinéti	[ʊʒraʃɪˈnʲeːtʲɪ]

TIME. CALENDAR

17. Weekdays

Monday	pirmãdienis (v)	[p'ɪr'ma:d'iɛn'ɪs]
Tuesday	antrãdienis (v)	[an'tra:d'iɛn'ɪs]
Wednesday	trečiãdienis (v)	[tr'ɛ'tʃ'æd'iɛn'ɪs]
Thursday	ketvirtãdienis (v)	[k'ɛtv'ɪr'ta:d'iɛn'ɪs]
Friday	penktãdienis (v)	[p'ɛŋk'ta:d'iɛn'ɪs]
Saturday	šeštãdienis (v)	[ʃɛʃ'ta:d'iɛn'ɪs]
Sunday	sekmãdienis (v)	[s'ɛk'ma:d'iɛn'ɪs]

today (adv)	šiañdien	['ʃænd'iɛn]
tomorrow (adv)	rytoj	[r'i:'toj]
the day after tomorrow	porýt	[po'r'i:t]
yesterday (adv)	vãkar	['va:kar]
the day before yesterday	užvakar	['uʒvakar]

day	dienà (m)	[d'iɛ'na]
working day	dárbo dienà (m)	['darbɔ d'iɛ'na]
public holiday	šveñtinė dienà (m)	['ʃvent'ɪn'e: d'iɛ'na]
day off	išeigìnė dienà (m)	[ɪʃɛɪ'g'ɪn'e: d'iɛ'na]
weekend	savaitgalis (v)	[sa'vʌɪtgal'ɪs]

all day long	vìsą diẽną	['v'ɪsa: 'd'ɛna:]
the next day (adv)	sèkančią diẽną	['s'ɛkantʃ'ɪæ: 'd'ɛna:]
two days ago	priẽš dvì dienàs	['pr'ɛʃ 'dv'ɪ d'iɛ'nas]
the day before	išvakarėse	['ɪʃvakar'e:se]
daily (adj)	kasdiẽnis	[kas'd'ɛn'ɪs]
every day (adv)	kasdiẽn	[kas'd'ɛn]

week	savaitė (m)	[sa'vʌɪt'e:]
last week (adv)	praeitą savaitę	['pra'ɛɪta: sa'vʌɪt'ɛ:]
next week (adv)	ateinančią savaitę	[a't'ɛɪnantʃ'æ: sa'vʌɪt'ɛ:]
weekly (adj)	kassavaitinis	[kassa'vʌɪt'ɪn'ɪs]
every week (adv)	kàs savaitę	['kas sa'vʌɪt'ɛ:]
twice a week	dù kartùs per savaitę	['du kar'tus p'ɛr sa'vʌɪt'ɛ:]
every Tuesday	kiekvíeną antrãdienį	[k'iɛk'v'ɪ:ɛna: an'tra:d'ɪ:ɛn'ɪ:]

18. Hours. Day and night

morning	rýtas (v)	['r'i:tas]
in the morning	rytè	[r'i:'t'ɛ]
noon, midday	vidùrdienis (v)	[v'ɪ'durd'iɛn'ɪs]
in the afternoon	popiẽt	[po'p'ɛt]

evening	vãkaras (v)	['va:karas]
in the evening	vakarè	[vaka'r'ɛ]

night	naktìs (m)	[nak'tʲɪs]
at night	nãktį	['na:kti:]
midnight	vidùrnaktis (v)	[vʲɪ'dʊrnaktʲɪs]

second	sekùndė (m)	[sʲɛ'kʊndʲe:]
minute	minùtė (m)	[mʲɪ'nʊtʲe:]
hour	valandà (m)	[valʲan'da]
half an hour	pùsvalandis (v)	['pʊsvalʲandʲɪs]
a quarter-hour	ketvìrtis valandõs	[kʲɛt'vʲɪrtʲɪs valʲan'do:s]
fifteen minutes	penkiólika minùčių	[pʲɛŋ'kʲolʲɪka mʲɪ'nʊtʂʲu:]
24 hours	parà (m)	[pa'ra]

sunrise	sáulės patekėjimas (v)	['saʊlʲe:s patʲɛ'kʲɛjɪmas]
dawn	aušrà (m)	[aʊʃ'ra]
early morning	ankstyvas rýtas (v)	[aŋk'stʲi:vas 'rʲi:tas]
sunset	saulėlydis (v)	[saʊ'lʲe:lʲi:dʲɪs]

early in the morning	ankstì rytè	[aŋk'stɪ rʲi:'tʲɛ]
this morning	šiañdien rytè	['ʃændʲiɛn rʲi:'tʲɛ]
tomorrow morning	rytój rytè	[rʲi:'toj rʲi:'tʲɛ]

this afternoon	šiañdien diẽną	['ʃæn'dʲɛn 'dʲiɛna:]
in the afternoon	popiẽt	[po'pʲɛt]
tomorrow afternoon	rytój popiẽt	[rʲi:'toj po'pʲɛt]

tonight (this evening)	šiañdien vakarè	['ʃændʲiɛn vaka'rʲɛ]
tomorrow night	rytój vakarè	[rʲi:'toj vaka'rʲɛ]

at 3 o'clock sharp	lýgiai trẽčią vãlandą	['lʲi:gʲɛɪ 'trʲætʂʲæ: 'va:landa:]
about 4 o'clock	apiẽ ketvìrtą vãlandą	[a'pʲɛ kʲɛtvʲɪrta: va:landa:]
by 12 o'clock	dvýliktai vãlandai	['dvʲi:lʲɪktʌɪ 'va:landʌɪ]

in 20 minutes	ùž dvidešimtiẽs minùčių	['ʊʒ dvʲɪdʲɛʃɪm'tʲɛs mʲɪ'nʊtʂʲu:]
in an hour	ùž valandõs	['ʊʒ valʲan'do:s]
on time (adv)	laikù	[lʲʌɪ'kʊ]

a quarter to ...	bè ketvìrčio	['bʲɛ 'kʲɛtvʲɪrtʂʲo]
within an hour	valandõs bėgyje	[valʲan'do:s 'bʲe:gʲi:je]
every 15 minutes	kàs penkiólika minùčių	['kas pʲɛŋ'kʲolʲɪka mʲɪ'nʊtʂʲu:]
round the clock	vìsą pãrą (m)	['vʲɪsa: 'pa:ra:]

19. Months. Seasons

January	saũsis (v)	['saʊsʲɪs]
February	vasãris (v)	[va'sa:rʲɪs]
March	kovàs (v)	[kɔ'vas]
April	balañdis (v)	[ba'lʲandʲɪs]
May	gegužė̃ (m)	[gʲɛgʊ'ʒʲe:]
June	biržẽlis (v)	[bʲɪr'ʒʲælʲɪs]

July	líepa (m)	['lʲiɛpa]
August	rugpjũtis (v)	[rʊg'pju:tʲɪs]
September	rugsė́jis (v)	[rʊg'sʲɛjɪs]
October	spãlis (v)	['spa:lʲɪs]

| November | lãpkritis (v) | ['lʲaːpkrʲɪtʲɪs] |
| December | grúodis (v) | ['gruadʲɪs] |

spring	pavãsaris (v)	[paˈvaːsarʲɪs]
in spring	pavãsarį	[paˈvaːsarʲɪː]
spring (as adj)	pavasarìnis	[pavasaˈrʲɪnʲɪs]

summer	vãsara (m)	['vaːsara]
in summer	vãsarą	['vaːsaraː]
summer (as adj)	vasarìnis	[vasaˈrʲɪnʲɪs]

autumn	ruduõ (v)	[ruˈdua]
in autumn	rùdenį	['rudʲɛnʲɪː]
autumn (as adj)	rudenìnis	[rudʲɛ'nʲɪnʲɪs]

winter	žiemà (m)	[ʒʲiɛ'ma]
in winter	žiẽmą	['ʒʲɛmaː]
winter (as adj)	žiemìnis	[ʒʲiɛ'mʲɪnʲɪs]

month	ménuo (v)	['mʲeːnua]
this month	šį ménesį	[ʃɪː 'mʲeːnesʲɪː]
next month	kìtą ménesį	['kʲɪːta: 'mʲeːnesʲɪː]
last month	praeitą ménesį	['praʲɛɪta: 'mʲeːnesʲɪː]

a month ago	priẽš ménesį	['prʲɪːɛʃ 'mʲeːnesʲɪː]
in a month (a month later)	ùž ménesio	['uʒ 'mʲeːnesʲɔ]
in 2 months (2 months later)	ùž dvejų̃ ménesių	['uʒ dve'ju: 'mʲeːnesʲuː]
the whole month	vìsą ménesį	['vʲɪsaː 'mʲeːnesʲɪː]
all month long	vìsą ménesį	['vʲɪsaː 'mʲeːnesʲɪː]

monthly (~ magazine)	kasménesìnis	[kasmʲeːne'sʲɪnʲɪs]
monthly (adv)	kàs ménesį	['kas 'mʲeːnesʲɪː]
every month	kiekvíeną ménesį	[kʲiɛk'vʲɪːɛna: 'mʲeːnesʲɪː]
twice a month	dù kartùs peĩ ménesį	['du karˈtus per 'mʲeːnesʲɪː]

year	mẽtai (v dgs)	['mʲætʌɪ]
this year	šiaĩs mẽtais	['ʃʲɛɪs 'mʲætʌɪs]
next year	kitaĩs mẽtais	[kʲɪ'tʌɪs 'mʲætʌɪs]
last year	praeitaĩs mẽtais	[praʲɛɪ'tʌɪs 'mʲætʌɪs]

a year ago	priẽš metùs	['prʲɛʃ mʲɛ'tus]
in a year	ùž mẽtų	['uʒ 'mʲætuː]
in two years	ùž dvejų̃ mẽtų	['uʒ dvʲɛ'ju: 'mʲætuː]
the whole year	visùs metùs	[vʲɪ'sus mʲɛ'tus]
all year long	visùs metùs	[vʲɪ'sus mʲɛ'tus]

every year	kàs metùs	['kas mʲɛ'tus]
annual (adj)	kasmetìnis	[kasmʲɛ'tʲɪnʲɪs]
annually (adv)	kàs metùs	['kas mʲɛ'tus]
4 times a year	kẽturis kartùs per metùs	['kʲæturʲɪs kar'tus pʲɛr mʲɛ'tus]

date (e.g. today's ~)	dienà (m)	[dʲiɛ'na]
date (e.g. ~ of birth)	datà (m)	[da'ta]
calendar	kalendõrius (v)	[kalʲɛn'do:rʲus]
half a year	pùsė mẽtų	['pusʲe: 'mʲætuː]

six months	**pusmetis** (v)	['pʊsmⁱɛtⁱɪs]
season (summer, etc.)	**sezonas** (v)	[sⁱɛ'zonas]
century	**ámžius** (v)	['amʒⁱʊs]

TRAVEL. HOTEL

20. Trip. Travel

tourism, travel	turìzmas (v)	[tʊ'rʲɪzmas]
tourist	turìstas (v)	[tʊ'rʲɪstas]
trip, voyage	keliõnė (m)	[kʲɛ'lʲo:nʲe:]
adventure	nuotykis (v)	['nʊatʲi:kʲɪs]
trip, journey	ìšvyka (m)	['ɪʃvʲi:ka]
holiday	atóstogos (m dgs)	[a'tostogos]
to be on holiday	atostogáuti	[atosto'gaʊtʲɪ]
rest	póilsis (v)	['poɪlʲsʲɪs]
train	traukinỹs (v)	[traʊkʲɪ'nʲi:s]
by train	tráukiniu	['traʊkʲɪnʲʊ]
aeroplane	léktuvas (v)	[lʲe:k'tʊvas]
by aeroplane	léktuvu	[lʲe:ktʊ'vʊ]
by car	automobiliù	[aʊtomobʲɪ'lʲʲʊ]
by ship	laivù	[lʲʲʌɪ'vʊ]
luggage	bagãžas (v)	[ba'ga:ʒas]
suitcase	lagamìnas (v)	[lʲaga'mʲɪnas]
luggage trolley	bagãžo vežimėlis (v)	[ba'ga:ʒɔ veʒʲɪ'mʲe:lʲɪs]
passport	pãsas (v)	['pa:sas]
visa	vìzà (m)	[vʲɪ'za]
ticket	bìlietas (v)	['bʲɪlʲiɛtas]
air ticket	léktuvo bìlietas (v)	[lʲe:k'tʊvɔ 'bʲɪlʲiɛtas]
guidebook	vadõvas (v)	[va'do:vas]
map (tourist ~)	žemélapis (v)	[ʒe'mʲe:lʲapʲɪs]
area (rural ~)	vietóvė (m)	[vʲiɛ'tovʲe:]
place, site	vietà (m)	[vʲiɛ'ta]
exotica (n)	egzòtika (m)	[ɛg'zotʲɪka]
exotic (adj)	egzòtinis	[ɛg'zotʲɪnʲɪs]
amazing (adj)	nuostabùs	[nʊasta'bʊs]
group	grùpė (m)	['grʊpʲe:]
excursion, sightseeing tour	ekskùrsija (m)	[ɛks'kʊrsʲɪjɛ]
guide (person)	ekskùrsijos vadõvas (v)	[ɛks'kʊrsʲɪjos va'do:vas]

21. Hotel

hotel	viẽšbutis (v)	['vʲɛʃbʊtʲɪs]
motel	motèlis (v)	[mo'tʲɛlʲɪs]
three-star (~ hotel)	3 žvaigždùtės	['trʲɪs ʒvʌɪgʒ'dʊtʲe:s]

five-star	5 žvaigždutės	['penⁱkⁱos ʒvʌɪgʒ'dutⁱe:s]
to stay (in a hotel, etc.)	apsistóti	[apsⁱɪs'totⁱɪ]

room	kambarỹs (v)	[kamba'rⁱi:s]
single room	vienvíetis kambarỹs (v)	['vⁱiɛn'vⁱɛtⁱɪs kamba'rⁱi:s]
double room	dvivíetis kambarỹs (v)	[dvⁱɪ'vⁱɛtⁱɪs kamba'rⁱi:s]
to book a room	rezervúoti kambarį	[rⁱɛzⁱɛr'vuatⁱɪ 'kambarⁱɪ:]

half board	pusiáu pensiónas (v)	[pusⁱæu pⁱɛnsⁱɪ'jonas]
full board	pensiónas (v)	[pⁱɛnsⁱɪ'jonas]

with bath	sù vonià	['su vo'nⁱæ]
with shower	sù dušù	['su dʊ'ʃu]
satellite television	palydõvinė televìzija (m)	[palⁱi:'do:vⁱɪnⁱe: tⁱɛlⁱɛ'vⁱɪzⁱɪjɛ]
air-conditioner	kondicioniẽrius (v)	[kondⁱɪtsⁱɪjo'nⁱɛrⁱus]
towel	rañkšluostis (v)	['raŋkʃlⁱuastⁱɪs]
key	rãktas (v)	['ra:ktas]

administrator	administrãtorius (v)	[admⁱɪnⁱɪs'tra:torⁱus]
chambermaid	kambarìnė (m)	[kamba'rⁱɪnⁱe:]
porter	nešìkas (v)	[nⁱɛ'ʃⁱɪkas]
doorman	registrãtorius (v)	[rⁱɛgⁱɪs'tra:torⁱus]

restaurant	restorãnas (v)	[rⁱɛsto'ra:nas]
pub, bar	bãras (v)	['ba:ras]
breakfast	pùsryčiai (v dgs)	['pusrⁱi:tʂⁱɛɪ]
dinner	vakariẽnė (m)	[vaka'rⁱɛnⁱe:]
buffet	švèdiškas stãlas (v)	['ʃvⁱɛdⁱɪʃkas 'sta:lⁱas]

lobby	vestibiùlis (v)	[vⁱɛstⁱɪ'bⁱulⁱɪs]
lift	lìftas (v)	['lⁱɪftas]

DO NOT DISTURB	NETRUKDÝTI	[nⁱɛtrʊk'dⁱi:tⁱɪ]
NO SMOKING	NERŪKÝTI!	[nⁱɛru:'kⁱi:tⁱɪ]

22. Sightseeing

monument	pamiñklas (v)	[pa'mⁱɪŋklⁱas]
fortress	tvirtóvė (m)	[tvⁱɪr'tovⁱe:]
palace	rū́mai (v)	['ru:mʌɪ]
castle	pilìs (m)	[pⁱɪ'lⁱɪs]
tower	bókštas (v)	['bokʃtas]
mausoleum	mauzoliẽjus (v)	[mauzo'lⁱɛjus]

architecture	architektūrà (m)	[arxⁱɪtⁱɛktu:'ra]
medieval (adj)	vidùramžių	[vⁱɪ'dʊramʒⁱu:]
ancient (adj)	senóvinis	[sⁱɛ'novⁱɪnⁱɪs]
national (adj)	nacionãlinis	[natsⁱɪjo'na:lⁱɪnⁱɪs]
famous (monument, etc.)	žymùs	[ʒⁱi:'mus]

tourist	turìstas (v)	[tʊ'rⁱɪstas]
guide (person)	gìdas (v)	['gⁱɪdas]
excursion, sightseeing tour	ekskùrsija (m)	[ɛks'kursⁱɪjɛ]
to show (vt)	ródyti	['rodⁱi:tⁱɪ]

to tell (vt)	pãsakoti	['pa:sakotʲɪ]
to find (vt)	rãsti	['rastʲɪ]
to get lost (lose one's way)	pasiklýsti	[pasʲɪ'klʲi:stʲɪ]
map (e.g. underground ~)	schemà (m)	[sxʲɛ'ma]
map (e.g. city ~)	plãnas (v)	['plʲa:nas]

souvenir, gift	suvenýras (v)	[sʊvʲɛ'nʲi:ras]
gift shop	suvenýrų parduotùvė (m)	[sʊve'nʲi:ru: pardʊɑ'tʊvʲe:]
to take pictures	fotografùoti	[fotogra'fʊɑtʲɪ]
to have one's picture taken	fotografùotis	[fotogra'fʊɑtʲɪs]

TRANSPORT

23. Airport

English	Lithuanian	Pronunciation
airport	óro úostas (v)	['orɔ 'uɑstas]
aeroplane	léktuvas (v)	[lʲe:k'tʊvas]
airline	aviakompãnija (m)	[avʲækom'pa:nʲɪjɛ]
air traffic controller	dispéčeris (v)	[dʲɪs'pʲɛtʂʲɛrʲɪs]
departure	išskridìmas (v)	[ɪʃskrʲɪ'dʲɪmas]
arrival	atskridìmas (v)	[atskrʲɪ'dʲɪmas]
to arrive (by plane)	atskrìsti	[ats'krʲɪstʲɪ]
departure time	išvykìmo laĩkas (v)	[ɪʃvʲi:'kʲɪmɔ 'lʲʌɪkas]
arrival time	atvykìmo laĩkas (v)	[atvʲi:'kʲɪmɔ 'lʲʌɪkas]
to be delayed	vėlúoti	[vʲe:'lʲuɑtʲɪ]
flight delay	skrỹdžio atidėjìmas (v)	['skrʲi:dʒʲɔ atʲɪdʲe:'jɪmas]
information board	informãcinė šviẽslentė (m)	[ɪnfor'ma:tsʲɪnʲe: 'ʃvʲɛslʲɛntʲe:]
information	informãcija (m)	[ɪnfor'ma:tsʲɪjɛ]
to announce (vt)	paskélbti	[pas'kʲɛlʲptʲɪ]
flight (e.g. next ~)	reĩsas (v)	['rʲɛɪsas]
customs	muĩtinė (m)	['mʊɪtʲɪnʲe:]
customs officer	muĩtininkas (v)	['mʊɪtʲɪnʲɪŋkas]
customs declaration	deklarãcija (m)	[dʲɛklʲa'ra:tsʲɪjɛ]
to fill in (vt)	užpìldyti	[ʊʒ'pʲɪlʲdʲi:tʲɪ]
to fill in the declaration	užpìldyti deklarãciją	[ʊʒ'pʲɪlʲdʲi:tʲɪ dʲɛkla'ra:tsɪja:]
passport control	pasų̃ kontrõlė (m)	[pa'su: kon'trolʲe:]
luggage	bagãžas (v)	[ba'ga:ʒas]
hand luggage	rañkinis bagãžas (v)	['raŋkʲɪnʲɪs ba'ga:ʒas]
luggage trolley	vežimė̃lis (v)	[vʲɛʒʲɪr'mʲe:lʲɪs]
landing	įlaipìnimas (v)	[i:lʲʌɪ'pʲɪ:nʲɪmas]
landing strip	nusileidìmo tãkas (v)	[nʊsʲɪlʲɛɪ'dʲɪmɔ ta:kas]
to land (vi)	léistis	['lʲɛɪstʲɪs]
airstair (passenger stair)	laiptẽliai (v dgs)	[lʌɪp'tʲælʲɛɪ]
check-in	registrãcija (m)	[rʲɛgʲɪs'tra:tsʲɪjɛ]
check-in counter	registrãcijos stãlas (v)	[rʲɛgʲɪs'tra:tsʲɪjɔs 'sta:lʲas]
to check-in (vi)	užsiregistrúoti	[ʊʒsʲɪrʲɛgʲɪs'trʊɑtʲɪ]
boarding card	įlipìmo talõnas (v)	[i:lʲɪ'pʲɪ:mɔ ta'lonas]
departure gate	išėjìmas (v)	[ɪʃʲe:'jɪmas]
transit	tranzìtas (v)	[tran'zʲɪtas]
to wait (vt)	láukti	['lʲɑʊktʲɪ]
departure lounge	laukiamãsis (v)	[lʲɑʊkʲæ'masʲɪs]

| to see off | lydėti | [lʲiːˈdʲeːtʲɪ] |
| to say goodbye | atsisveikinti | [atsʲɪˈsvʲɛɪkʲɪntʲɪ] |

24. Aeroplane

aeroplane	lėktùvas (v)	[lʲeːkˈtʊvas]
air ticket	lėktùvo bìlietas (v)	[lʲeːkˈtʊvɔ ˈbʲɪlʲiɛtas]
airline	aviakompãnija (m)	[avʲækomˈpaːnʲɪjɛ]
airport	óro ùostas (v)	[ˈorɔ ˈʊostas]
supersonic (adj)	viršgarsìnis	[vʲɪrʃɡarˈsʲɪnʲɪs]

captain	órlaivio kapitõnas (v)	[ˈorlʲʌɪvʲɔ kapʲɪˈtoːnas]
crew	ekipãžas (v)	[ɛkʲɪˈpaːʒas]
pilot	pilòtas (v)	[pʲɪˈlʲotas]
stewardess	stiuardėsė (m)	[stʲʊarˈdʲɛsʲeː]
navigator	štùrmanas (v)	[ˈʃtʊrmanas]

wings	sparnaĩ (v dgs)	[sparˈnʌɪ]
tail	gãlas (v)	[ˈɡaːlʲas]
cockpit	kabinà (m)	[kabʲɪˈna]
engine	varìklis (v)	[vaˈrʲɪklʲɪs]
undercarriage (landing gear)	važiuõklė (m)	[vaʒʲʊˈoːklʲeː]
turbine	turbinà (m)	[tʊrbʲɪˈna]
propeller	propèleris (v)	[proˈpʲɛlʲɛrʲɪs]
black box	juodà dėžė (m)	[jʊɒˈda dʲeːˈʒʲeː]
yoke (control column)	vairãratis (v)	[vʌɪˈraːratʲɪs]
fuel	degalaĩ (v dgs)	[dʲɛɡaˈlʲʌɪ]

safety card	instrùkcija (m)	[ɪnsˈtrʊktsʲɪjɛ]
oxygen mask	deguõnies káukė (m)	[dʲɛɡʊɒˈnʲiɛs ˈkaʊkʲe:]
uniform	unifòrma (m)	[ʊnʲɪˈforma]
lifejacket	gélbėjimosi liemẽnė (m)	[ˈɡʲælʲbʲeːjimosʲɪ lʲiɛˈmʲænʲeː]
parachute	parašiùtas (v)	[paraˈʃʊtas]
takeoff	kilìmas (v)	[kʲɪˈlʲɪmas]
to take off (vi)	kìlti	[ˈkʲɪlʲtʲɪ]
runway	kilìmo tãkas (v)	[kʲɪˈlʲɪmɔ ˈtaːkas]

visibility	matomùmas (v)	[matoˈmʊmas]
flight (act of flying)	skrỹdis (v)	[ˈskrʲiːdʲɪs]
altitude	aũkštis (v)	[ˈɒʊkʃtʲɪs]
air pocket	óro duobė̃ (m)	[ˈorɔ dʊɒˈbʲeː]

seat	vietà (m)	[vʲiɛˈta]
headphones	ausìnės (m dgs)	[ɒʊˈsʲɪnʲeːs]
folding tray (tray table)	atverčiamàsis staliùkas (v)	[atvʲɛrtʃʲæˈmasʲɪs staˈlʲʊkas]
airplane window	iliuminãtorius (v)	[ɪlʲʊmʲɪˈnaːtorʲʊs]
aisle	praėjìmas (v)	[praeːˈjɪmas]

25. Train

| train | traukinỹs (v) | [trɒʊkʲɪˈnʲiːs] |
| commuter train | elektrìnis traukinỹs (v) | [ɛlʲɛkˈtrʲɪnʲɪs trɒʊkʲɪˈnʲiːs] |

express train	greitasis traukinys (v)	[grɪɛɪ'tasʲɪs traʊkʲɪ'nʲiːs]
diesel locomotive	motorvežis (v)	[mo'torvʲɛʒʲɪs]
steam locomotive	garvežys (v)	[garvʲɛ'ʒʲiːs]

coach, carriage	vagonas (v)	[va'gonas]
buffet car	vagonas restoranas (v)	[va'gonas rʲɛsto'raːnas]

rails	bėgiai (v dgs)	['bʲeːgʲɛɪ]
railway	geležinkelis (v)	[gʲɛlʲɛ'ʒʲɪŋkʲɛlʲɪs]
sleeper (track support)	pabėgis (v)	['paːbʲeːgʲɪs]

platform (railway ~)	platforma (m)	[plʲat'forma]
platform (~ 1, 2, etc.)	kelias (v)	['kʲælʲæs]
semaphore	semaforas (v)	[sʲɛma'foras]
station	stotis (m)	[sto'tʲɪs]
train driver	mašinistas (v)	[maʃɪ'nʲɪstas]
porter (of luggage)	nešikas (v)	[nʲɛ'ʃɪkas]
carriage attendant	konduktorius (v)	[kɔn'duktorʲʊs]
passenger	keleivis (v)	[kʲɛ'lʲɛɪvʲɪs]
ticket inspector	kontrolierius (v)	[kɔntro'lʲɛrʲʊs]

corridor (in train)	koridorius (v)	[kɔ'rʲɪdorʲʊs]
emergency brake	stabdymo kranas (v)	['sta:bdʲiːmɔ 'kraːnas]

compartment	kupė (m)	[kʊ'pʲeː]
berth	lentyna (m)	[lʲɛn'tʲiːna]
upper berth	viršutinė lentyna (m)	[vʲɪrʃʊ'tʲɪnʲeː lʲɛn'tʲiːna]
lower berth	apatinė lentyna (m)	[apa'tʲɪnʲeː lʲɛn'tʲiːna]
bed linen, bedding	patalynė (m)	['pa:talʲiːnʲeː]
ticket	bilietas (v)	['bʲɪlʲɪɛtas]
timetable	tvarkaraštis (v)	[tvar'ka:raʃtʲɪs]
information display	šviešlentė (m)	['ʃvʲɛslʲɛntʲeː]

to leave, to depart	išvykti	[ɪʃ'vʲiːktʲɪ]
departure (of a train)	išvykimas (v)	[ɪʃvʲiː'kʲɪmas]
to arrive (ab. train)	atvykti	[at'vʲiːktʲɪ]
arrival	atvykimas (v)	[atvʲiː'kʲɪmas]

to arrive by train	atvažiuoti traukiniu	[atva'ʒʲʊatʲɪ 'traʊkʲɪnʲʊ]
to get on the train	įlipti į traukinį	[i:'lʲɪːptʲɪ iː 'traʊkʲɪnʲɪː]
to get off the train	išlipti iš traukinio	[ɪʃ'lʲɪːptʲɪ ɪʃ 'traʊkʲɪnʲɔ]

train crash	katastrofa (m)	[katastro'fa]
to derail (vi)	nulėkti nuo bėgių	[nʊ'lʲeːktʲɪ 'nʊa 'bʲeːgʲuː]

steam locomotive	garvežys (v)	[garvʲɛ'ʒʲiːs]
stoker, fireman	kūrikas (v)	[ku:'rʲɪkas]
firebox	kūrykla (m)	[ku:rʲɪk'lʲa]
coal	anglis (m)	[ang'lʲɪs]

26. Ship

ship	laivas (v)	['lʲaɪvas]
vessel	laivas (v)	['lʲaɪvas]

steamship	gárlaivis (v)	['garlʲʌɪvʲɪs]
riverboat	motòrlaivis (v)	[mo'torlʲʌɪvʲɪs]
cruise ship	láineris (v)	['lʲʌɪnʲɛrʲɪs]
cruiser	kreìseris (v)	['krʲɛɪsʲɛrʲɪs]

yacht	jachtà (m)	[jax'ta]
tugboat	vilkìkas (v)	[vʲɪlʲ'kʲɪkas]
barge	bárža (m)	['barʒa]
ferry	kéltas (v)	['kʲɛlʲtas]

| sailing ship | bùrinis laĩvas (v) | ['bʊrʲɪnʲɪs 'lʲʌɪvas] |
| brigantine | brigantinà (m) | [brʲɪgantʲɪ'na] |

| ice breaker | lèdlaužis (v) | ['lʲædlɑʊʒʲɪs] |
| submarine | povandenìnis laĩvas (v) | [povandʲɛ'nʲɪnʲɪs 'lʲʌɪvas] |

boat (flat-bottomed ~)	váltis (m)	['valʲtʲɪs]
dinghy (lifeboat)	váltis (m)	['valʲtʲɪs]
lifeboat	gélbėjimo váltis (m)	['gʲælʲbʲe:jɪmɔ 'valʲtʲɪs]
motorboat	káteris (v)	['ka:tʲɛrʲɪs]

captain	kapitõnas (v)	[kapʲɪ'to:nas]
seaman	jūreĩvis (v)	[ju:'rʲɛɪvʲɪs]
sailor	jū́rininkas (v)	['ju:rʲɪnʲɪŋkas]
crew	ekipãžas (v)	[ɛkʲɪ'pa:ʒas]

boatswain	bòcmanas (v)	['botsmanas]
ship's boy	jùnga (m)	['jʊnga]
cook	virėjas (v)	[vʲɪ'rʲe:jas]
ship's doctor	laĩvo gýdytojas (v)	['lʲʌɪvɔ 'gʲi:dʲi:to:jɛs]

deck	dẽnis (v)	['dʲænʲɪs]
mast	stíebas (v)	['stʲiɛbas]
sail	bùrė (m)	['bʊrʲe:]

hold	triùmas (v)	['trʲʊmas]
bow (prow)	laĩvo príekis (v)	['lʲʌɪvɔ 'prʲiɛkʲɪs]
stern	laivãgalis (v)	[lʌɪ'va:galʲɪs]
oar	ìrklas (v)	['ɪrklʲas]
screw propeller	sraĩgtas (v)	['srʌɪktas]

cabin	kajùtė (m)	[ka'jʊtʲe:]
wardroom	kajutkompãnija (m)	[kajʊtkom'pa:nʲɪjɛ]
engine room	mašìnų skỹrius (v)	[ma'ʃɪnu 'skʲi:rʲʊs]
bridge	kapitõno tiltẽlis (v)	[kapʲɪ'to:nɔ tʲɪlʲ'tʲælʲɪs]
radio room	rãdijo kabinà (m)	['ra:dʲɪjɔ kabʲɪ'na]
wave (radio)	bangà (m)	[ban'ga]
logbook	laĩvo žurnãlas (v)	['lʲʌɪvɔ ʒʊr'na:lʲas]

spyglass	žiūrõnas (v)	[ʒʲu:'ro:nas]
bell	laĩvo skaȗbalas (v)	['lʲʌɪvɔ 'skambalʲas]
flag	vėliava (m)	['vʲe:lʲæva]

hawser (mooring ~)	lýnas (v)	['lʲi:nas]
knot (bowline, etc.)	mãzgas (v)	['ma:zgas]
deckrails	turėklai (v dgs)	[tʊ'rʲe:klʲʌɪ]

gangway	trāpas (v)	['tra:pas]
anchor	iñkaras (v)	['ɪŋkaras]
to weigh anchor	pakelti iñkarą	[pa'kʲɛlʲtʲɪ 'ɪŋkara:]
to drop anchor	nuleisti iñkarą	[nʊ'lʲɛɪstʲɪ 'iŋkara:]
anchor chain	iñkaro grandinė (m)	['ɪŋkarɔ gran'dʲɪnʲe:]

port (harbour)	uostas (v)	['ʊɑstas]
quay, wharf	prieplauka (m)	['prʲiɛplʲɑʊka]
to berth (moor)	prisišvartuoti	[prʲɪsʲɪʃvar'tʊɑtʲɪ]
to cast off	išplaukti	[ɪʃplʲɑʊktʲɪ]

trip, voyage	kelionė (m)	[kʲɛ'lʲo:nʲe:]
cruise (sea trip)	kruizas (v)	[krʊ'ɪzas]
course (route)	kursas (v)	['kʊrsas]
route (itinerary)	maršrutas (v)	[marʃrʊtas]

fairway (safe water channel)	farvateris (v)	[far'va:tʲɛrʲɪs]
shallows	seklumà (m)	[sʲɛklʲʊ'ma]
to run aground	užplaukti ant seklumõs	[ʊʒ'plʲɑʊktʲɪ ant sʲɛklʲʊ'mo:s]

storm	audrà (m)	[ɑʊd'ra]
signal	signãlas (v)	[sʲɪg'na:lʲas]
to sink (vi)	skęsti	['skʲɛ:stʲɪ]
Man overboard!	Žmogùs vandenyjè!	[ʒmo'gʊs vandʲɛnʲi:'jæ!]
SOS (distress signal)	SOS	[ɛs ɔ ɛs]
ring buoy	gélbėjimosi rãtas (v)	[gʲɛlʲbʲe:jimosʲɪ 'ra:tas]

CITY

27. Urban transport

bus, coach	autobùsas (v)	[auto'busas]
tram	tramvãjus (v)	[tram'va:jus]
trolleybus	troleibùsas (v)	[trolʲɛɪ'busas]
route (bus ~)	maršrùtas (v)	[marʃrutas]
number (e.g. bus ~)	nùmeris (v)	['numʲɛrʲɪs]

to go by ...	važiúoti ...	[va'ʒʲuatʲɪ ...]
to get on (~ the bus)	įlìpti į̃ ...	[i:'lʲɪːptʲɪ i: ...]
to get off ...	išlìpti ìš ...	[ɪʃ'lʲɪptʲɪ ɪʃ ...]

stop (e.g. bus ~)	stotēlė (m)	[sto'tʲælʲeː]
next stop	kità stotēlė (m)	[kʲɪ'ta sto'tʲælʲe:]
terminus	galutìnė stotēlė (m)	[galu'tʲɪnʲe: sto'tʲælʲe:]
timetable	tvarkãraštis (v)	[tvar'ka:raʃtʲɪs]
to wait (vt)	láukti	['lʲauktʲɪ]

ticket	bìlietas (v)	['bʲɪlʲiɛtas]
fare	bìlieto káina (m)	['bʲɪlʲiɛto 'kʌɪna]

cashier (ticket seller)	kãsininkas (v)	['ka:sʲɪnʲɪŋkas]
ticket inspection	kontrolė̃ (m)	[kɔn'trolʲe:]
ticket inspector	kontroliẽrius (v)	[kɔntro'lʲɛrʲus]

to be late (for ...)	vėlúoti	[vʲe:'lʲuatʲɪ]
to miss (~ the train, etc.)	pavėlúoti	[pavʲe:'lʲuatʲɪ]
to be in a hurry	skubéti	[skʊ'bʲe:tʲɪ]

taxi, cab	taksì (v)	[tak'sʲɪ]
taxi driver	taksìstas (v)	[tak'sʲɪstas]
by taxi	sù taksì	['sʊ tak'sʲɪ]
taxi rank	taksì stovéjimo aikštēlė (m)	[tak'sʲɪ sto'vʲɛjɪmɔ ʌɪkʃ'tʲælʲe:]
to call a taxi	iškviẽsti taksì	[ɪʃk'vʲɛstʲɪ tak'sʲɪ]
to take a taxi	įsėstì į̃ taksì	[i:sʲes'tʲɪ: i: tak'sʲɪ:]

traffic	gãtvės judéjimas (v)	['ga:tvʲe:s jʊ'dʲɛjɪmas]
traffic jam	kamštìs (v)	['kamʃtʲɪs]
rush hour	pìko vãlandos (m dgs)	['pʲɪkɔ 'va:lʲandos]
to park (vi)	parkúotis	[par'kuatʲɪs]
to park (vt)	parkúoti	[par'kuatʲɪ]
car park	stovéjimo aikštēlė (m)	[sto'vʲɛjɪmɔ ʌɪkʃ'tʲælʲe:]

underground, tube	metrò	[mʲɛ'tro]
station	stotìs (m)	[sto'tʲɪs]
to take the tube	važiúoti metrò	[va'ʒʲuatʲɪ mʲɛ'tro]
train	traukinỹs (v)	[traʊkʲɪ'nʲi:s]
train station	stotìs (m)	[sto'tʲɪs]

28. City. Life in the city

city, town	miestas (v)	['mʲɛstas]
capital city	sóstinė (m)	['sostʲɪnʲe:]
village	káimas (v)	['kʌɪmas]

city map	miesto plãnas (v)	['mʲɛstɔ 'plʲa:nas]
city centre	miesto ceñtras (v)	['mʲɛstɔ 'tsʲɛntras]
suburb	príemiestis (v)	['prʲiɛmʲɛstʲɪs]
suburban (adj)	príemiesčio	['prʲiɛmʲiɛstʃʲɔ]

outskirts	pakraštỹs (v)	[pakraʃ'tʲi:s]
environs (suburbs)	apýlinkės (m dgs)	[a'pʲi:lʲɪŋkʲe:s]
city block	kvartãlas (v)	[kvar'ta:lʲas]
residential block (area)	gyvẽnamas kvartãlas (v)	[gʲi:'vʲænamas kvar'ta:lʲas]

traffic	judėjimas (v)	[juˈdʲɛjɪmas]
traffic lights	šviesofòras (v)	[ʃvʲiɛso'foras]
public transport	miesto transpòrtas (v)	['mʲɛstɔ trans'portas]
crossroads	sánkryža (m)	['saŋkrʲi:ʒa]

zebra crossing	pérėja (m)	['pʲɛrʲe:ja]
pedestrian subway	požeminė pérėja (m)	[poʒe'mʲɪnʲe: 'pʲærʲe:ja]
to cross (~ the street)	péreiti	['pʲɛrʲɛɪtʲɪ]
pedestrian	pėstysis (v)	['pʲe:stʲi:sʲɪs]
pavement	šaligatvis (v)	[ʃa'lʲɪgatvʲɪs]

| bridge | tìltas (v) | ['tʲɪlʲtas] |
| embankment (river walk) | krantìnė (m) | [kran'tʲɪnʲe:] |

allée (garden walkway)	aléja (m)	[a'lʲe:ja]
park	párkas (v)	['parkas]
boulevard	bulvãras (v)	[bʊlʲi'va:ras]
square	aikštė̃ (m)	[ʌɪkʃ'tʲe:]
avenue (wide street)	prospèktas (v)	[pros'pʲɛktas]
street	gãtvė (m)	['ga:tvʲe:]
side street	skersgatvis (v)	['skʲɛrsgatvʲɪs]
dead end	tupìkas (v)	[tʊ'pʲɪkas]

house	nãmas (v)	['na:mas]
building	pãstatas (v)	['pa:statas]
skyscraper	dangóraižis (v)	[dan'gorʌɪʒʲɪs]

facade	fasãdas (v)	[fa'sa:das]
roof	stógas (v)	['stogas]
window	lángas (v)	['lʲangas]
arch	árka (m)	['arka]
column	kolonà (m)	[kɔlʲo'na]
corner	kampas (v)	['kampas]

shop window	vitrinà (m)	[vʲɪtrʲɪ'na]
signboard (store sign, etc.)	ìškaba (m)	['ɪʃkaba]
poster (e.g., playbill)	afišà (m)	[afʲɪ'ʃa]
advertising poster	reklãminis plakãtas (v)	[rʲɛk'lʲa:mʲɪnʲɪs plʲa'ka:tas]
hoarding	reklãminis skỹdas (v)	[rʲɛk'lʲa:mʲɪnʲɪs 'skʲi:das]

rubbish	šiukšlės (m dgs)	['ʃʊkʃˡeːs]
rubbish bin	urna (m)	['ʊrna]
to litter (vi)	šiukšlinti	['ʃʊkʃˡɪntˡɪ]
rubbish dump	sąvartynas (v)	[saːvarˡtˡiːnas]

telephone box	telefono budelė (m)	[tˡɛlˡɛ'fonɔ 'bʊdelˡe:]
lamppost	žibinto stulpas (v)	[ʒɪˡr'bˡɪntɔ 'stʊlˡpas]
bench (park ~)	suolas (v)	['sʊalˡas]

police officer	policininkas (v)	[po'lˡɪtsˡɪnˡɪŋkas]
police	policija (m)	[po'lˡɪtsˡɪjɛ]
beggar	skurdžius (v)	['skʊrdʒˡʊs]
homeless (n)	benamis (v)	[bˡɛ'naːmˡɪs]

29. Urban institutions

shop	parduotuvė (m)	[pardʊa'tʊvˡe:]
chemist, pharmacy	vaistinė (m)	['vʌɪstˡɪnˡe:]
optician (spectacles shop)	optika (m)	['optˡɪka]
shopping centre	prekybos centras (v)	[prˡɛ'kˡi:bos 'tsˡɛntras]
supermarket	supermarketas (v)	[sʊpˡɛr'markˡɛtas]

bakery	bandelių krautuvė (m)	[ban'dˡælˡu: 'krautʊvˡe:]
baker	kepėjas (v)	[kˡɛ'pˡe:jas]
cake shop	konditerija (m)	[kɔndˡɪ'tˡɛrˡɪjɛ]
grocery shop	bakalėja (m)	[baka'lˡe:ja]
butcher shop	mėsos krautuvė (m)	[mˡe:'so:s 'krautʊvˡe:]

| greengrocer | daržovių krautuvė (m) | [dar'ʒovˡu: 'krautʊvˡe:] |
| market | prekyvietė (m) | [prˡɛ'kˡi:vˡiɛtˡe:] |

coffee bar	kavinė (m)	[ka'vˡɪnˡe:]
restaurant	restoranas (v)	[rˡɛsto'ra:nas]
pub, bar	aludė (m)	[a'lˡʊdˡe:]
pizzeria	picerija (m)	[pˡɪ'tsˡɛrˡɪjɛ]

hairdresser	kirpykla (m)	[kˡɪrpˡi:k'lˡa]
post office	paštas (v)	['pa:ʃtas]
dry cleaners	valykla (m)	[valˡi:k'la]
photo studio	fotoateljė (v)	[fotoate'lˡje:]

shoe shop	avalynės parduotuvė (m)	['a:valˡi:nˡe:s pardʊa'tʊvˡe:]
bookshop	knygynas (v)	[knˡiː'gˡi:nas]
sports shop	sportinių prekių parduotuvė (m)	['sportˡɪnˡu: 'prˡækˡu: pardʊa'tʊvˡe:]

clothes repair shop	drabužių taisykla (m)	[dra'bʊʒˡu: tʌɪsˡi:k'lˡa]
formal wear hire	drabužių nuoma (m)	[dra'bʊʒˡu: 'nʊama]
video rental shop	filmų nuoma (m)	['fˡɪlˡmu: 'nʊama]

circus	cirkas (v)	['tsˡɪrkas]
zoo	zoologijos sodas (v)	[zoo'lˡogˡɪjɔs 'so:das]
cinema	kino teatras (v)	['kˡɪnɔ tˡɛ'a:tras]
museum	muziejus (v)	[mʊ'zˡɛjʊs]

library	biblioteka (m)	[bʲɪblʲɪjɔtʲɛ'ka]
theatre	teātras (v)	[tʲɛ'a:tras]
opera (opera house)	opera (m)	['opʲɛra]
nightclub	naktìnis klùbas (v)	[nak'tʲɪnʲɪs 'klʲubas]
casino	kazino (v)	[kazʲɪ'no]

mosque	mečetė (m)	[mʲɛ'tʂʲɛtʲe:]
synagogue	sinagoga (m)	[sʲɪnago'ga]
cathedral	kātedra (m)	['ka:tʲɛdra]
temple	šventykla (m)	[ʃvʲɛntʲiːk'lʲa]
church	bažnyčia (m)	[baʒ'nʲiːtʂʲæ]

college	institùtas (v)	[ɪnstʲɪ'tutas]
university	universitētas (v)	[unʲɪvʲɛrsʲɪ'tʲɛtas]
school	mokykla (m)	[mokʲiːk'lʲa]

prefecture	prefektūra (m)	[prʲɛfʲɛk'tu:'ra]
town hall	savivaldybė (m)	[savʲɪvalʲʲdʲi:bʲe:]
hotel	viešbutis (v)	['vʲɛʃbutʲɪs]
bank	bánkas (v)	['baŋkas]

embassy	ambasada (m)	[ambasa'da]
travel agency	turìzmo agentūra (m)	[tu'rʲɪzmɔ agʲɛntu:'ra]
information office	informācijos biùras (v)	[ɪnfor'ma:tsʲɪjɔs 'bʲuras]
currency exchange	keitykla (m)	[kʲɛɪtʲi:k'lʲa]

underground, tube	metro	[mʲɛ'tro]
hospital	ligóninė (m)	[lʲɪ'gonʲɪnʲe:]

petrol station	degalìnė (m)	[dʲɛga'lʲɪnʲe:]
car park	stovėjimo aikštēlė (m)	[sto'vʲɛjɪmɔ ʌɪkʃ'tʲælʲe:]

30. Signs

signboard (store sign, etc.)	ìškaba (m)	['ɪʃkaba]
notice (door sign, etc.)	ùžrašas (v)	['uʒraʃas]
poster	plakātas (v)	[plʲa'ka:tas]
direction sign	núoroda (m)	['nuaroda]
arrow (sign)	rodyklė (m)	[ro'dʲi:klʲe:]

caution	pérspėjimas (v)	['pʲɛrspʲe:jimas]
warning sign	įspėjìmas (v)	[i:spʲe:'jɪmas]
to warn (vt)	įspéti	[i:s'pʲe:tʲɪ]

rest day (weekly ~)	išeigìnė dienà (m)	[ɪʃɛɪ'gʲɪnʲe: dʲiɛ'na]
timetable (schedule)	tvarkāraštis (v)	[tvar'ka:raʃtʲɪs]
opening hours	dárbo valandõs (m dgs)	['darbɔ valʲan'do:s]

WELCOME!	SVEIKÌ ATVŸKĘ!	[svʲɛɪ'kʲɪ at'vʲiːkʲe:!]
ENTRANCE	ĮĖJÌMAS	[i:ʲɛ:'jɪmas]
WAY OUT	IŠĖJÌMAS	[ɪʃʲe:'jɪmas]

PUSH	STÙMTI	['stumtʲɪ]
PULL	TRÁUKTI	['traʊktʲɪ]

| OPEN | ATIDARÝTA | [atʲɪda'rʲiːta] |
| CLOSED | UŽDARÝTA | [ʊʒda'rʲiːta] |

| WOMEN | MÓTERIMS | ['motʲɛrʲɪms] |
| MEN | VÝRAMS | ['vʲiːrams] |

DISCOUNTS	NÚOLAIDOS	['nʊalʲʌɪdos]
SALE	IŠPARDAVÌMAS	[ɪʃparda'vʲɪmas]
NEW!	NAUJÍENA!	[nɑʊ'jiɛna!]
FREE	NEMÓKAMAI	[nʲɛ'mokamʌɪ]

ATTENTION!	DĖMESIO!	['dʲeːmesʲɔ!]
NO VACANCIES	VIĖTŲ NĖRA	['vʲɛtuː 'nʲeːra]
RESERVED	REZERVÚOTA	[rʲɛzʲɛr'vʊata]

| ADMINISTRATION | ADMINISTRÁCIJA | [admʲɪnʲɪs'tratsʲɪja] |
| STAFF ONLY | TÌK PERSONÁLUI | ['tʲɪk pʲɛrso'nalʲʊi] |

BEWARE OF THE DOG!	PIKTAS ŠUO	['pʲɪktas 'ʃʊa]
NO SMOKING	RŪKÝTI DRAŪDŽIAMA	[ru:'kʲi:tʲɪ 'drɑʊdʒʲæma]
DO NOT TOUCH!	NELIĖSTI!	[nʲɛ'lʲɛstʲɪ!]

DANGEROUS	PAVOJÌNGA	[pavo'jɪnga]
DANGER	PAVÕJUS	[pa'voːjʊs]
HIGH VOLTAGE	AUKŠTÀ ĮTAMPA	[ɑʊkʃ'ta 'iːtampa]
NO SWIMMING!	MÁUDYTIS DRAŪDŽIAMA	['mɑʊdʲiːtʲɪs 'drɑʊdʒʲæma]
OUT OF ORDER	NEVEĨKIA	[nʲɛ'vʲɛɪkʲɛ]

FLAMMABLE	DEGÙ	[dʲɛ'gʊ]
FORBIDDEN	DRAŪDŽIAMA	['drɑʊdʒʲæma]
NO TRESPASSING!	PRAĖJÌMAS	[prae:'jɪmas
	DRAŪDŽIAMAS	'drɑʊdʒʲæmas]
WET PAINT	NUDAŽYTA	[nʊda'ʒʲiːta]

31. Shopping

to buy (purchase)	pìrkti	['pʲɪrktʲɪ]
shopping	pirkinỹs (v)	[pʲɪrkʲɪ'nʲiːs]
to go shopping	apsipìrkti	[apsʲɪ'pʲɪrktʲɪ]
shopping	apsipirkìmas (v)	[apsʲɪpʲɪr'kʲɪmas]

| to be open (ab. shop) | veĩkti | ['vʲɛɪktʲɪ] |
| to be closed | užsidarýti | [ʊʒsʲɪda'rʲiːtʲɪ] |

footwear, shoes	ãvalynė (m)	['aːvalʲiːnʲeː]
clothes, clothing	drabùžiai (v)	[dra'bʊʒʲɛɪ]
cosmetics	kosmètika (m)	[kɔs'mʲɛtʲɪka]
food products	prodùktai (v)	[pro'dʊktʌɪ]
gift, present	dovanà (m)	[dova'na]

shop assistant (masc.)	pardavéjas (v)	[parda'vʲeːjas]
shop assistant (fem.)	pardavéja (m)	[parda'vʲeːja]
cash desk	kasà (m)	[ka'sa]
mirror	veĩdrodis (v)	['vʲɛɪdrodʲɪs]

41

| counter (shop ~) | prekýstalis (v) | [prʲɛ'kʲiːstalʲɪs] |
| fitting room | matāvimosi kabinà (m) | [ma'taːvʲɪmosʲɪ kabʲɪ'na] |

to try on	matúoti	[ma'tʊatʲɪ]
to fit (ab. dress, etc.)	tìkti	['tʲɪktʲɪ]
to fancy (vt)	patìkti	[pa'tʲɪktʲɪ]

price	kaina (m)	['kʌɪna]
price tag	kainýnas (v)	[kʌɪ'nʲiːnas]
to cost (vt)	kainúoti	[kʌɪ'nʊatʲɪ]
How much?	Kíek?	['kʲiɛk?]
discount	núolaida (m)	['nʊalʲʌɪda]

inexpensive (adj)	nebrangùs	[nʲɛbran'gʊs]
cheap (adj)	pigùs	[pʲɪ'gʊs]
expensive (adj)	brangùs	[bran'gʊs]
It's expensive	Taì brangù.	['tʌɪ bran'gʊ]

hire (n)	núoma (m)	['nʊama]
to hire (~ a dinner jacket)	išsinúomoti	[ɪʃsʲɪ'nʊamotʲɪ]
credit (trade credit)	kreditas (v)	[krʲɛ'dʲɪtas]
on credit (adv)	kreditù	[krʲɛdʲɪ'tʊ]

CLOTHING & ACCESSORIES

32. Outerwear. Coats

clothes	apranga (m)	[apran'ga]
outerwear	viršutiniai drabužiai (v dgs)	[vʲɪrʃʊ'tʲɪnʲɛɪ dra'bʊʒʲɛɪ]
winter clothing	žieminiai drabužiai (v)	[ʒʲiɛ'mʲɪnʲɛɪ dra'bʊʒʲɛɪ]

coat (overcoat)	páltas (v)	['palʲtas]
fur coat	kailiniai (v dgs)	[kʌɪlʲɪ'nʲɛɪ]
fur jacket	puskailiniai (v)	['pʊskʌɪlʲɪnʲɛɪ]
down coat	pūkinė (m)	[puː'kʲɪnʲeː]

jacket (e.g. leather ~)	striukė (m)	['strʲʊkʲeː]
raincoat (trenchcoat, etc.)	apsiaustas (v)	[ap'sʲɛʊstas]
waterproof (adj)	neperšlampamas	[nʲɛ'pʲɛrʃlʲampamas]

33. Men's & women's clothing

shirt (button shirt)	marškiniai (v dgs)	[marʃkʲɪ'nʲɛɪ]
trousers	kelnės (m dgs)	['kʲɛlʲnʲeːs]
jeans	džinsai (v dgs)	['dʒʲɪnsʌɪ]
suit jacket	švarkas (v)	['ʃvarkas]
suit	kostiumas (v)	[kɔs'tʲʊmas]

dress (frock)	suknelė (m)	[sʊk'nʲælʲeː]
skirt	sijonas (v)	[sʲɪ'jɔːnas]
blouse	palaidinė (m)	[palʲʌɪ'dʲɪnʲeː]
knitted jacket (cardigan, etc.)	susegamas megztinis (v)	['sʊsʲɛgamas mʲɛgz'tʲɪnʲɪs]
jacket (of a woman's suit)	žaketas, švarkelis (v)	[ʒa'kʲɛtas], [ʃvar'kʲælʲɪs]

T-shirt	futbolininko marškiniai (v)	['fʊtbolʲɪnʲɪŋkɔ marʃkʲɪ'nʲɛɪ]
shorts (short trousers)	šortai (v dgs)	['ʃortʌɪ]
tracksuit	sportinis kostiumas (v)	['sportʲɪnʲɪs kɔs'tʲʊmas]
bathrobe	chalatas (v)	[xa'lʲaːtas]
pyjamas	pižama (m)	[pʲɪʒa'ma]

| jumper (sweater) | nertinis (v) | [nʲɛr'tʲɪnʲɪs] |
| pullover | megztinis (v) | [mʲɛgz'tʲɪnʲɪs] |

waistcoat	liemenė (m)	[lʲiɛ'mʲænʲeː]
tailcoat	frakas (v)	['fraːkas]
dinner suit	smokingas (v)	['smokʲɪngas]

uniform	uniforma (m)	[ʊnʲɪ'forma]
workwear	darbo drabužiai (v)	['darbɔ dra'bʊʒʲɛɪ]
boiler suit	kombinezonas (v)	[kɔmbʲɪnʲɛ'zonas]
coat (e.g. doctor's smock)	chalatas (v)	[xa'lʲaːtas]

34. Clothing. Underwear

underwear	baltiniai (v dgs)	[balʲtʲɪ'nʲɛɪ]
vest (singlet)	apatiniai marškinėliai (v dgs)	[apa'tʲɪnʲɛɪ marʃkʲɪ'nʲe:lʲɛɪ]
socks	kojinės (m dgs)	['ko:jɪnʲe:s]
nightdress	naktiniai marškiniai (v dgs)	[nak'tʲɪnʲɛɪ marʃkʲɪ'nʲɛɪ]
bra	liemenėlė (m)	[lʲɛme'nʲe:lʲe:]
knee highs (knee-high socks)	golfai (v)	['golʲfʌɪ]
tights	pėdkelnės (m dgs)	['pʲe:dkʲɛlʲnʲe:s]
stockings (hold ups)	kojinės (m dgs)	['ko:jɪnʲe:s]
swimsuit, bikini	maudymosi kostiumėlis (v)	['mɑʊdʲi:mosʲɪ kostʲʊ'mʲe:lʲɪs]

35. Headwear

hat	kepurė (m)	[kʲɛ'pʊrʲe:]
trilby hat	skrybėlė (m)	[skrʲi:bʲe:'lʲe:]
baseball cap	beisbolo lazda (m)	['bʲɛɪsbolʲɔ lʲaz'da]
flatcap	kepurė (m)	[kʲɛ'pʊrʲe:]
beret	beretė (m)	[bʲɛ'rʲɛtʲe:]
hood	gobtuvas (v)	[gop'tʊvas]
panama hat	panama (m)	[pana'ma]
knit cap (knitted hat)	megzta kepuraitė (m)	[mʲɛgz'ta kepʊ'rʌɪtʲe:]
headscarf	skara (m), skarelė (m)	[ska'ra], [ska'rʲælʲe:]
women's hat	skrybėlaitė (m)	[skrʲi:bʲe:'lʲʌɪtʲe:]
hard hat	šalmas (v)	['ʃalʲmas]
forage cap	pilotė (m)	[pʲɪ'lʲotʲe:]
helmet	šalmas (v)	['ʃalʲmas]
bowler	katiliukas (v)	[katʲɪ'lʲʊkas]
top hat	cilindras (v)	[tsʲɪ'lʲɪndras]

36. Footwear

footwear	avalynė (m)	['a:valʲi:nʲe:]
shoes (men's shoes)	batai (v)	['ba:tʌɪ]
shoes (women's shoes)	bateliai (v)	[ba'tʲælʲɛɪ]
boots (e.g., cowboy ~)	auliniai batai (v)	[ɑʊ'lʲɪnʲɛɪ 'ba:tʌɪ]
carpet slippers	šlepetės (m dgs)	[ʃlʲɛ'pʲætʲe:s]
trainers	sportbačiai (v dgs)	['sportbatʂʲɛɪ]
trainers	sportbačiai (v dgs)	['sportbatʂʲɛɪ]
sandals	sandalai (v dgs)	[san'da:lʲʌɪ]
cobbler (shoe repairer)	batsiuvys (v)	[batsʲʊ'vʲi:s]
heel	kulnas (v)	['kʊlʲnas]
pair (of shoes)	pora (m)	[po'ra]
lace (shoelace)	batraištis (v)	['ba:trʌɪʃtʲɪs]

to lace up (vt)	várstyti	['varstʲiːtʲɪ]
shoehorn	šáukštas (v)	['ʃɑʊkʃtas]
shoe polish	ãvalynės krèmas (v)	['aːvalʲiːnʲeːs 'krʲɛmas]

37. Personal accessories

gloves	pìrštinės (m dgs)	['pʲɪrʃtʲɪnʲeːs]
mittens	kùmštinės (m dgs)	['kʊmʃtʲɪnʲeːs]
scarf (muffler)	šãlikas (v)	['ʃaːlʲɪkas]

glasses	akiniaĩ (dgs)	[akʲɪ'nʲɛɪ]
frame (eyeglass ~)	rėmēliai (v dgs)	[rʲeː'mʲælʲɛɪ]
umbrella	skētis (v)	['skʲeːtʲɪs]
walking stick	lazdēlė (m)	[laz'dʲælʲeː]
hairbrush	plaukų̃ šepetỹs (v)	[plʲɑʊ'ku: ʃɛpʲɛ'tʲiːs]
fan	vėduõklė (m)	[vʲe:'dʊɑklʲe:]

tie (necktie)	kaklãraištis (v)	[kak'lʲaːrʌɪʃtʲɪs]
bow tie	petelìškė (m)	[pʲɛtʲɛ'lʲɪʃkʲe:]
braces	pētnešos (m dgs)	['pʲætnʲɛʃos]
handkerchief	nósinė (m)	['nosʲɪnʲe:]

comb	šùkos (m dgs)	['ʃʊkos]
hair slide	segtùkas (v)	[sʲɛk'tʊkas]
hairpin	plaukų̃ segtùkas (v)	[plʲɑʊ'ku: sʲɛk'tʊkas]
buckle	sagtìs (m)	[sak'tʲɪs]

belt	dìržas (v)	['dʲɪrʒas]
shoulder strap	dìržas (v)	['dʲɪrʒas]

bag (handbag)	rankinùkas (v)	[raŋkʲɪ'nʊkas]
handbag	rankinùkas (v)	[raŋkʲɪ'nʊkas]
rucksack	kuprìnė (m)	[kʊ'prʲɪnʲe:]

38. Clothing. Miscellaneous

fashion	madà (m)	[ma'da]
in vogue (adj)	madìngas	[ma'dʲɪngas]
fashion designer	modeliúotojas (v)	[modʲɛ'lʲʊɑtoːjɛs]

collar	apýkaklė (m)	[a'pʲiːkaklʲe:]
pocket	kišénė (m)	[kʲɪ'ʃænʲe:]
pocket (as adj)	kišenìnis	[kʲɪʃɛ'nʲɪnʲɪs]
sleeve	rankóvė (m)	[raŋ'kovʲe:]
hanging loop	pakabà (m)	[paka'ba]
flies (on trousers)	klỹnas (v)	['klʲiːnas]

zip (fastener)	užtrauktùkas (v)	[ʊʒtrɑʊk'tʊkas]
fastener	užsegìmas (v)	[ʊʒsʲɛ'gʲɪmas]
button	sagà (m)	[sa'ga]
buttonhole	kìlpa (m)	['kʲɪlʲpa]
to come off (ab. button)	atplýšti	[at'plʲiːʃtʲɪ]

to sew (vi, vt)	siúti	['sʲuːtʲɪ]
to embroider (vi, vt)	siuvinéti	[sʲuvʲɪ'nʲeːtʲɪ]
embroidery	siuvinéjimas (v)	[sʲuvʲɪ'nʲɛjɪmas]
sewing needle	ádata (m)	['aːdata]
thread	siúlas (v)	['sʲuːlʲas]
seam	siúlė (m)	['sʲuːlʲeː]

to get dirty (vi)	išsitépti	[ɪʃsʲɪ'tʲɛptʲɪ]
stain (mark, spot)	dėmė̃ (m)	[dʲeː'mʲeː]
to crease, to crumple	susiglámžyti	[susʲɪ'glʲa mʒʲiːtʲɪ]
to tear, to rip (vt)	suplė́šyti	[sup'lʲeːʃɪːtʲɪ]
clothes moth	kandis (v)	['kandʲɪs]

39. Personal care. Cosmetics

toothpaste	dantų̃ pastà (m)	[dan'tuː pas'ta]
toothbrush	dantų̃ šepetė́lis (v)	[dan'tuː ʃepe'tʲeːlʲɪs]
to clean one's teeth	valýti dantìs	[va'lʲiːtʲɪ dan'tʲɪs]

razor	skustùvas (v)	[sku'stuvas]
shaving cream	skutìmosi krèmas (v)	[sku'tʲɪmosʲɪ 'krʲɛmas]
to shave (vi)	skùstis	['skustʲɪs]

| soap | muĩlas (v) | ['muɪlʲas] |
| shampoo | šampū̃nas (v) | [ʃam'puːnas] |

scissors	žìrklės (m dgs)	['ʒɪrklʲeːs]
nail file	dìldė (m) nagáms	['dʲɪlʲdʲe: na'gams]
nail clippers	gnybtùkai (v)	[gnʲiːp'tukʌɪ]
tweezers	pincètas (v)	[pʲɪn'tsʲɛtas]

cosmetics	kosmètika (m)	[kɔs'mʲɛtʲɪka]
face mask	kaũkė (m)	['kaukʲe:]
manicure	manikiū̃ras (v)	[manʲɪ'kʲuːras]
to have a manicure	darýti manikiū̃rą	[da'rʲiːtʲɪ manʲɪ'kʲuːraː]
pedicure	pedikiū̃ras (v)	[pʲɛdʲɪ'kʲuːras]

make-up bag	kosmètinė (m)	[kɔs'mʲɛtʲɪnʲe:]
face powder	pudrà (m)	[pud'ra]
powder compact	pùdrinė (m)	['pudrʲɪnʲe:]
blusher	skaistalaĩ (v dgs)	[skʌɪsta'lʲaĩ]

perfume (bottled)	kvepalaĩ (v dgs)	[kvʲɛpa'lʲaĩ]
toilet water (lotion)	tualètinis vanduõ (v)	[tua'lʲɛtʲɪnʲɪs van'duɑ]
lotion	losjònas (v)	[lʲo'sjɔ nas]
cologne	odekolònas (v)	[odʲɛko'lʲonas]

eyeshadow	vokų̃ šešéliai (v)	[vo'kuː ʃe'ʃʲe:lʲɛɪ]
eyeliner	akių̃ pieštùkas (v)	[a'kʲuː pʲɪɛʃ'tukas]
mascara	tùšas (v)	['tuʃas]

lipstick	lū́pų dažaĩ (v)	['lʲuːpu da'ʒʌɪ]
nail polish	nagų̃ lãkas (v)	[na'gu 'lʲaːkas]
hair spray	plaukų̃ lãkas (v)	[plʲau'ku: 'lʲaːkas]

deodorant	dezodorántas (v)	[dˈɛzodoˈrantas]
cream	krėmas (v)	[ˈkrʲɛmas]
face cream	véido krėmas (v)	[ˈvʲɛɪdɔ ˈkrʲɛmas]
hand cream	rañkų krėmas (v)	[ˈraŋku: ˈkrʲɛmas]
anti-wrinkle cream	krėmas (v) nuõ raukšlių̃	[ˈkrʲɛmas nʊɑ rɑʊkʃˈlʲʊ:]
day cream	dieninis krėmas (v)	[dʲiɛˈnʲɪnʲɪs ˈkrʲɛmas]
night cream	naktìnis krėmas (v)	[nakˈtʲɪnʲɪs ˈkrʲɛmas]
day (as adj)	dieninis	[dʲiɛˈnʲɪnʲɪs]
night (as adj)	naktìnis	[nakˈtʲɪnʲɪs]

tampon	tampónas (v)	[tamˈponas]
toilet paper (toilet roll)	tualetinis pópierius (v)	[tʊaˈlʲɛtʲɪnʲɪs ˈpo:pʲiɛrʲʊs]
hair dryer	fėnas (v)	[ˈfʲɛnas]

40. Watches. Clocks

watch (wristwatch)	laĩkrodis (v)	[ˈlʲʌɪkrodʲɪs]
dial	ciferblãtas (v)	[tsʲɪfʲɛrˈblʲa:tas]
hand (clock, watch)	rodýklė (m)	[roˈdʲi:klʲe:]
metal bracelet	apýrankė (m)	[aˈpʲi:raŋkʲe:]
watch strap	diržẽlis (v)	[dʲɪrˈʒʲælʲɪs]

battery	elemeñtas (v)	[ɛlʲɛˈmʲɛntas]
to be flat (battery)	išsikráuti	[ɪʃsʲɪˈkrɑʊtʲɪ]
to change a battery	pakeĩsti elemeñtą	[paˈkʲɛɪstʲɪ ɛlʲɛˈmʲɛnta:]
to run fast	skubéti	[skʊˈbʲe:tʲɪ]
to run slow	atsilìkti	[atsʲɪˈlʲɪktʲɪ]

wall clock	síeninis laĩkrodis (v)	[ˈsʲiɛnʲɪnʲɪs ˈlʲʌɪkrodʲɪs]
hourglass	smẽlio laĩkrodis (v)	[ˈsmʲeːlʲɔ ˈlʌɪkrodʲɪs]
sundial	sáulės laĩkrodis (v)	[ˈsɑʊlʲeːs ˈlʌɪkrodʲɪs]
alarm clock	žadintùvas (v)	[ʒadʲɪnˈtʊvas]
watchmaker	laĩkrodininkas (v)	[ˈlʲʌɪkrodʲɪnʲɪŋkas]
to repair (vt)	taisýti	[tʌɪˈsʲi:tʲɪ]

47

EVERYDAY EXPERIENCE

41. Money

money	pinigaĩ (v)	[pʲɪnʲɪˈgʌɪ]
currency exchange	keitìmas (v)	[kʲɛɪˈtʲɪmas]
exchange rate	kùrsas (v)	[ˈkʊrsas]
cashpoint	bankomãtas (v)	[baŋkoˈmaːtas]
coin	monetà (m)	[monʲɛˈta]
dollar	dòleris (v)	[ˈdolʲɛrʲɪs]
euro	eũras (v)	[ˈɛʊras]
lira	lirà (m)	[lʲɪˈra]
Deutschmark	márkė (m)	[ˈmarkʲeː]
franc	fránkas (v)	[ˈfraŋkas]
pound sterling	svãras (v)	[ˈsvaːras]
yen	jenà (m)	[jɛˈna]
debt	skolà (m)	[skoˈlʲa]
debtor	skõlininkas (v)	[ˈskoːlʲɪnʲɪŋkas]
to lend (money)	dúoti į̃ skõlą	[ˈdʊatʲɪ iː ˈskoːlʲaː]
to borrow (vi, vt)	im̃ti į̃ skõlą	[ˈɪmtʲɪ iː ˈskoːlʲaː]
bank	bánkas (v)	[ˈbaŋkas]
account	sąskaità (m)	[ˈsaːskʌɪta]
to deposit into the account	dė́ti į̃ sąskaità̃	[ˈdʲeːtʲɪ iː ˈsaːskʌɪta]
to withdraw (vt)	im̃ti iš sąskaitos	[ˈɪmtʲɪ ɪʃ ˈsaːskʌɪtos]
credit card	kredìtinė kortẽlė (m)	[krʲɛˈdʲɪtʲɪnʲeː korˈtʲælʲeː]
cash	grynìeji pinigaĩ (v)	[grʲiːˈnʲiɛjɪ pʲɪnʲɪˈgʌɪ]
cheque	čẽkis (v)	[ˈtʂʲɛkʲɪs]
to write a cheque	išrašýti čẽkį	[ɪʃraˈʃiːtʲɪ ˈtʂʲɛkʲiː]
chequebook	čẽkių knygẽlė (m)	[ˈtʂʲɛkʲuː knʲiːˈgʲælʲeː]
wallet	piniginė̃ (m)	[pʲɪnʲɪˈgʲɪnʲeː]
purse	piniginė̃ (m)	[pʲɪnʲɪˈgʲɪnʲeː]
safe	seĩfas (v)	[ˈsʲɛɪfas]
heir	paveldė́tojas (v)	[pavelʲˈdʲeːtoːjɛs]
inheritance	palikìmas (v)	[palʲɪˈkʲɪmas]
fortune (wealth)	tur̃tas (v)	[ˈtʊrtas]
lease	núoma (m)	[ˈnʊama]
rent (money)	bùto mókestis (v)	[ˈbʊto ˈmokʲɛstʲɪs]
to rent (sth from sb)	núomotis	[ˈnʊamotʲɪs]
price	káina (m)	[ˈkʌɪna]
cost	káina (m)	[ˈkʌɪna]
sum	sumà (m)	[sʊˈma]

to spend (vt)	**léisti**	['lʲɛɪstʲɪ]
expenses	**są́naudos** (m dgs)	['sa:nɑʊdos]
to economize (vi, vt)	**taupýti**	[tɑʊ'pʲi:tʲɪ]
economical	**taupùs**	[tɑʊ'pʊs]
to pay (vi, vt)	**mokéti**	[mo'kʲe:tʲɪ]
payment	**apmokéjimas** (v)	[apmo'kʲɛjɪmas]
change (give the ~)	**grąžà** (m)	[gra:'ʒa]
tax	**mókestis** (v)	['mokʲɛstʲɪs]
fine	**baudà** (m)	[bɑʊ'da]
to fine (vt)	**baũsti**	['bɑʊstʲɪ]

42. Post. Postal service

post office	**pãštas** (v)	['pa:ʃtas]
post (letters, etc.)	**pãštas** (v)	['pa:ʃtas]
postman	**pãštininkas** (v)	['pa:ʃtʲɪnʲɪŋkas]
opening hours	**dárbo valandõs** (m dgs)	['darbɔ valʲan'do:s]
letter	**láiškas** (v)	['lʲʌɪʃkas]
registered letter	**užsakýtas láiškas** (v)	[ʊʒsa'kʲi:tas 'lʲʌɪʃkas]
postcard	**atvirùtė** (m)	[atvʲɪ'rʊtʲe:]
telegram	**telegramà** (m)	[tʲɛlʲɛgra'ma]
parcel	**siuntinỹs** (v)	[sʲʊntʲɪ'nʲi:s]
money transfer	**piniginis pavedìmas** (v)	[pʲɪnʲɪ'gʲɪnʲɪs pavʲɛ'dʲɪmas]
to receive (vt)	**gáuti**	['gɑʊtʲɪ]
to send (vt)	**išsių̃sti**	[ɪʃ'sʲu:stʲɪ]
sending	**išsiuntìmas** (v)	[ɪʃsʲʊn'tʲɪmas]
address	**ãdresas** (v)	['a:drʲɛsas]
postcode	**iñdeksas** (v)	['ɪndʲɛksas]
sender	**siuntéjas** (v)	[sʲʊn'tʲe:jas]
receiver	**gavéjas** (v)	[ga'vʲe:jas]
name (first name)	**var̃das** (v)	['vardas]
surname (last name)	**pavardẽ** (m)	[pavar'dʲe:]
postage rate	**tarìfas** (v)	[ta'rʲɪfas]
standard (adj)	**į̃prastas**	['i:prastas]
economical (adj)	**taupùs**	[tɑʊ'pʊs]
weight	**svõris** (v)	['svo:rʲɪs]
to weigh (~ letters)	**sver̃ti**	['svʲɛrtʲɪ]
envelope	**võkas** (v)	['vo:kas]
postage stamp	**markùtė** (m)	[mar'kʊtʲe:]

43. Banking

bank	**bánkas** (v)	['baŋkas]
branch (of a bank)	**skỹrius** (v)	['skʲi:rʲʊs]

| consultant | konsultántas (v) | [kɔnsʊlʲˈtantas] |
| manager (director) | valdýtojas (v) | [valʲˈdʲiːtoːjɛs] |

bank account	są́skaita (m)	[ˈsaːskʌɪta]
account number	są́skaitos númeris (v)	[ˈsaːskʌɪtos ˈnʊmʲɛrʲɪs]
current account	einamóji są́skaita (m)	[ɛɪnaˈmoːjɪ ˈsaːskʌɪta]
deposit account	kaupiamóji są́skaita (m)	[kɑʊpʲæˈmoːjɪ ˈsaːskʌɪta]

to open an account	atidarýti są́skaitą	[atʲɪdaˈrʲiːtʲɪ ˈsaːskʌɪtaː]
to close the account	uždarýti są́skaitą	[ʊʒdaˈrʲiːtʲɪ ˈsaːskʌɪtaː]
to deposit into the account	padéti į̃ są́skaitą	[paˈdʲeːtʲɪ iː ˈsaːskʌɪtaː]
to withdraw (vt)	paimti iš są́skaitos	[ˈpʌɪmtʲɪ ɪʃ ˈsaːskʌɪtos]

deposit	iñdėlis (v)	[ˈɪndʲeːlʲɪs]
to make a deposit	įnešti iñdėlį	[iːˈnʲɛʃtʲɪ ˈindʲeːlʲɪː]
wire transfer	pavedìmas (v)	[pavʲɛˈdʲɪmas]
to wire, to transfer	atlìkti pavedìmą	[atʲˈlʲɪktʲɪ pavʲɛˈdʲɪmaː]

| sum | sumà (m) | [sʊˈma] |
| How much? | Kíek? | [ˈkʲiɛk?] |

| signature | pãrašas (v) | [ˈpaːraʃas] |
| to sign (vt) | pasirašýti | [pasʲɪraˈʃʲɪːtʲɪ] |

credit card	kreditinė kortelė (m)	[krʲɛˈdʲɪtʲɪnʲeː korˈtʲælʲeː]
code (PIN code)	kòdas (v)	[ˈkodas]
credit card number	kreditinės kortelės númeris (v)	[krʲɛˈdʲɪtʲɪnʲeːs korˈtʲælʲeːs ˈnʊmerʲɪs]
cashpoint	bankomãtas (v)	[baŋkoˈmaːtas]

cheque	kvìtas (v)	[ˈkvʲɪtas]
to write a cheque	išrašýti kvìtą	[ɪʃraˈʃʲiːtʲɪ ˈkvʲɪtaː]
chequebook	čekių knygẽlė (m)	[ˈtʂɛkʲuː knʲiːˈgʲælʲeː]

loan (bank ~)	kreditas (v)	[krʲɛˈdʲɪtas]
to apply for a loan	kreiptis dėl kredito	[ˈkrʲɛɪptʲɪs dʲeːlʲ krʲɛˈdʲɪtɔ]
to get a loan	imti kreditą	[ˈɪmtʲɪ krʲɛˈdʲɪtaː]
to give a loan	suteikti kreditą	[sʊˈtʲɛɪktʲɪ krʲɛˈdʲɪtaː]
guarantee	garántija (m)	[gaˈrantʲɪjɛ]

44. Telephone. Phone conversation

telephone	telefónas (v)	[tʲɛlʲɛˈfonas]
mobile phone	mobilùsis telefónas (v)	[mobʲɪˈlʊsʲɪs tʲɛlʲɛˈfonas]
answerphone	autoatsakìklis (v)	[ɑʊtoatsaˈkʲɪklʲɪs]

| to call (by phone) | skambìnti | [ˈskambʲɪntʲɪ] |
| call, ring | skambùtis (v) | [skamˈbʊtʲɪs] |

to dial a number	suriñkti númerį	[sʊˈrʲɪŋktʲɪ ˈnʊmʲɛrʲɪː]
Hello!	Aliõ!	[aˈlʲɪo!]
to ask (vt)	pakláusti	[pakˈlʲɑʊstʲɪ]
to answer (vi, vt)	atsakýti	[atsaˈkʲiːtʲɪ]
to hear (vt)	girdéti	[gʲɪrˈdʲeːtʲɪ]

well (adv)	geraĩ	[gʲɛ'rʌɪ]
not well (adv)	prastaĩ	[pras'tʌɪ]
noises (interference)	trukdžiaĩ (v dgs)	[trʊk'dʒʲɛɪ]

receiver	ragẽlis (v)	[ra'gʲælʲɪs]
to pick up (~ the phone)	pakélti ragẽlį	[pa'kʲɛlʲtʲɪ ra'gʲælʲɪ:]
to hang up (~ the phone)	padéti ragẽlį	[pa'dʲe:tʲɪ ra'gʲælʲɪ:]

busy (engaged)	ùžimtas	['ʊʒʲɪmtas]
to ring (ab. phone)	skambéti	[skam'bʲe:tʲɪ]
telephone book	telefõnų knygà (m)	[tʲɛlʲɛ'fonu: knʲi:'ga]

local (adj)	viẽtinis	['vʲiɛtʲɪnʲɪs]
local call	viẽtinis skambùtis (v)	['vʲiɛtʲɪnʲɪs skam'bʊtʲɪs]
trunk (e.g. ~ call)	tarpmiestìnis	[tarpmʲiɛs'tʲɪnʲɪs]
trunk call	tarpmiestìnis skambùtis (v)	[tarpmʲiɛs'tʲɪnʲɪs skam'bʊtʲɪs]
international (adj)	tarptautìnis	[tarptɑʊ'tʲɪnʲɪs]
international call	tarptautìnis skambùtis (v)	[tarptɑʊ'tʲɪnʲɪs skam'bʊtʲɪs]

45. Mobile telephone

mobile phone	mobilùsis telefõnas (v)	[mobʲɪ'lʊsʲɪs tʲɛlʲɛ'fonas]
display	ekrãnas (v)	[ɛk'ra:nas]
button	mygtùkas (v)	[mʲi:k'tʊkas]
SIM card	SIM-kortẽlė (m)	[sʲɪm-kor'tʲælʲe:]

battery	akumuliãtorius (v)	[akʊmʊ'lʲætorʲʊs]
to be flat (battery)	išsikráuti	[ɪʃsʲɪ'krɑʊtʲɪ]
charger	įkrovìklis (v)	[i:kro'vʲɪ:klʲɪs]

menu	valgiãraštis (v)	[valʲ'gʲæraʃtʲɪs]
settings	nustãtymai (v dgs)	[nʊ'sta:tʲi:mʌɪ]
tune (melody)	melõdija (m)	[mʲɛ'lʲodʲɪjɛ]
to select (vt)	pasiriñkti	[pasʲɪ'rʲɪŋktʲɪ]

calculator	skaičiuotùvas (v)	[skʌɪtʃʲʊo'tʊvas]
voice mail	baĩso pãštas (v)	['balʲsɔ 'pa:ʃtas]
alarm clock	žadintùvas (v)	[ʒadʲɪn'tʊvas]
contacts	telefõnų knygà (m)	[tʲɛlʲɛ'fonu: knʲi:'ga]

| SMS (text message) | SMS žinùtė (m) | [ɛsɛ'mɛs ʒʲɪnʊtʲe:] |
| subscriber | aboneñtas (v) | [abo'nʲɛntas] |

46. Stationery

| ballpoint pen | automãtinis šratinùkas (v) | [ɑʊto'ma:tʲɪnʲɪs ʃratʲɪ'nʊkas] |
| fountain pen | plunksnãkotis (v) | [plʲʊŋk'sna:kotʲɪs] |

pencil	pieštùkas (v)	[pʲiɛʃ'tʊkas]
highlighter	žymẽklis (v)	[ʒʲi:'mʲæklʲɪs]
felt-tip pen	flomãsteris (v)	[flʲo'ma:stʲɛrʲɪs]
notepad	bloknòtas (v)	[blʲok'notas]

diary	dienoraštis (v)	[dʲiɛ'noraʃtʲɪs]
ruler	liniuotė (m)	[lʲɪ'nʲʊoːtʲeː]
calculator	skaičiuotuvas (v)	[skʌɪtʂʲʊo'tʊvas]
rubber	trintukas (v)	[trʲɪn'tʊkas]
drawing pin	smeigtukas (v)	[smʲɛɪk'tʊkas]
paper clip	sąvaržėlė (m)	[saːvar'ʒʲeːlʲeː]

glue	klijai (v dgs)	[klʲɪ'jʌɪ]
stapler	segiklis (v)	[sʲɛ'gʲɪklʲɪs]
hole punch	skylamušis (v)	[skʲiː'lʲa:mʊʃʲɪs]
pencil sharpener	drožtukas (v)	[droʒ'tʊkas]

47. Foreign languages

language	kalba (m)	[kalʲˠba]
foreign (adj)	užsienio	['ʊʒsʲiɛnʲɔ]
foreign language	užsienio kalba (m)	['ʊʒsʲiɛnʲɔ kalʲba]
to study (vt)	studijuoti	[stʊdʲɪ'jʊatʲɪ]
to learn (language, etc.)	mokytis	['mokʲiː:tʲɪs]

to read (vi, vt)	skaityti	[skʌɪ'tʲiː:tʲɪ]
to speak (vi, vt)	kalbėti	[kalʲˠbʲeː:tʲɪ]
to understand (vt)	suprasti	[sʊp'rastʲɪ]
to write (vt)	rašyti	[ra'ʃɪː:tʲɪ]

fast (adv)	greitai	['grʲɛɪtʌɪ]
slowly (adv)	lėtai	[lʲeː:'tʌɪ]
fluently (adv)	laisvai	[lʲʌɪs'vʌɪ]

rules	taisyklės (m dgs)	[tʌɪ'sʲiː:klʲeː:s]
grammar	gramatika (m)	[gra'ma:tʲɪka]
vocabulary	leksika (m)	['lʲɛksʲɪka]
phonetics	fonetika (m)	[fo'nʲɛtʲɪka]

textbook	vadovėlis (v)	[vado'vʲeː:lʲɪs]
dictionary	žodynas (v)	[ʒo'dʲiː:nas]
teach-yourself book	savimokos vadovėlis (v)	[sa'vʲɪmokos vado'vʲeː:lʲɪs]
phrasebook	pasikalbėjimų knygelė (m)	[pasʲɪkalʲˠbʲɛjɪmu: knʲiː'gʲælʲeː:]

cassette, tape	kasetė (m)	[ka'sʲɛtʲeː:]
videotape	vaizdajuostė (m)	[vʌɪz'da:jʊostʲeː:]
CD, compact disc	kompaktinis diskas (v)	[kɔm'pa:ktʲɪnʲɪs 'dʲɪskas]
DVD	DVD diskas (v)	[dʲɪvʲɪ'dʲɪ dʲɪs'kas]

alphabet	abėcėlė (m)	[abʲeː:'tsʲeː:lʲeː:]
to spell (vt)	sakyti paraidžiui	[sa'kʲiː:tʲɪ parʌɪ'dʒʲʊɪ]
pronunciation	tarimas (v)	[ta'rʲɪmas]

accent	akcentas (v)	[ak'tsʲɛntas]
with an accent	su akcentu	['sʊ aktsʲɛn'tʊ]
without an accent	be akcento	['bʲɛ ak'tsʲɛntɔ]

word	žodis (v)	['ʒoːdʲɪs]
meaning	prasmė (m)	[pras'mʲeː:]

course (e.g. a French ~)	kùrsai (v dgs)	['kʊrsʌɪ]
to sign up	užsirašýti	[ʊʒsʲɪra'ʃɪːtʲɪ]
teacher	déstytojas (v)	['dʲeːstʲiːtoːjɛs]
translation (process)	vertìmas (v)	[vʲɛr'tʲɪmas]
translation (text, etc.)	vertìmas (v)	[vʲɛr'tʲɪmas]
translator	vertéjas (v)	[vʲɛr'tʲeːjas]
interpreter	vertéjas (v)	[vʲɛr'tʲeːjas]
polyglot	poliglòtas (v)	[polʲɪ'glotas]
memory	atmintìs (m)	[atmʲɪn'tʲɪs]

MEALS. RESTAURANT

48. Table setting

spoon	šáukštas (v)	['ʃɑʊkʃtas]
knife	peĩlis (v)	['pʲɛɪlʲɪs]
fork	šakùtė (m)	[ʃaˈkʊtʲeː]

cup (e.g., coffee ~)	puodùkas (v)	[pʊɑˈdʊkas]
plate (dinner ~)	lėkštė̃ (m)	[lʲeːkʃˈtʲeː]
saucer	lėkštẽlė (m)	[lʲeːkʃˈtʲælʲeː]
serviette	servetė̃lė (m)	[sʲɛrveˈtʲeːlʲeː]
toothpick	dantų̃ krapštùkas (v)	[danˈtuː krapʃˈtʊkas]

49. Restaurant

restaurant	restorãnas (v)	[rʲɛstoˈraːnas]
coffee bar	kavìnė (m)	[kaˈvʲɪnʲeː]
pub, bar	bãras (v)	['baːras]
tearoom	arbãtos salònas (v)	[arˈbaːtos saˈlʲonas]

waiter	padavė́jas (v)	[padaˈvʲeːjas]
waitress	padavė́ja (m)	[padaˈvʲeːja]
barman	bármenas (v)	['barmʲɛnas]

menu	meniù (v)	[mʲɛˈnʲʊ]
wine list	vỹnų žemė́lapis (v)	['vʲiːnu ʒeˈmʲeːlʲapʲɪs]
to book a table	rezervúoti staliùką	[rʲɛzʲɛrˈvʊɑtʲɪ staˈlʲʊkaː]

course, dish	pãtiekalas (v)	['paːtʲiɛkalʲas]
to order (meal)	užsisakýti	[ʊʒsʲɪsakʲiːtʲɪ]
to make an order	padarýti užsãkymą	[padaˈrʲiːtʲɪ ʊʒˈsaːkʲiːmaː]

aperitif	aperitỹvas (v)	[apʲɛrʲɪˈtʲiːvas]
starter	ùžkandis (v)	['ʊʒkandʲɪs]
dessert, pudding	desèrtas (v)	[dʲɛˈsʲɛrtas]

bill	sąskaita (m)	['saːskʌɪta]
to pay the bill	apmokė́ti sąskaitą	[apmoˈkʲeːtʲɪ 'saːskʌɪtaː]
to give change	dúoti grąžõs	['dʊɑtʲɪ graːˈʒoːs]
tip	arbãtpinigiai (v dgs)	[arˈbaːtpʲɪnʲɪgʲɛɪ]

50. Meals

| food | válgis (v) | ['valʲgʲɪs] |
| to eat (vi, vt) | válgyti | ['valʲgʲiːtʲɪ] |

breakfast	pusryčiai (v dgs)	['pʊsrʲiːtʃʲɛɪ]
to have breakfast	pusryčiauti	['pʊsrʲiːtʃʲɛʊtʲɪ]
lunch	pietūs (v)	['pʲɛ'tuːs]
to have lunch	pietáuti	[pʲɛ'tɑʊtʲɪ]
dinner	vakarienė (m)	[vaka'rʲɛnʲeː]
to have dinner	vakarieniáuti	[vakarʲiɛ'nʲæʊtʲɪ]

| appetite | apetitas (v) | [apʲɛ'tʲɪtas] |
| Enjoy your meal! | Gero apetito! | ['gʲærɔ apʲɛ'tʲɪtɔ!] |

to open (~ a bottle)	atidaryti	[atʲɪda'rʲiːtʲɪ]
to spill (liquid)	išpilti	[ɪʃ'pʲɪlʲtʲɪ]
to spill out (vi)	išsipilti	[ɪʃsʲɪ'pʲɪlʲtʲɪ]

to boil (vi)	virti	['vʲɪrtʲɪ]
to boil (vt)	virinti	['vʲɪrʲɪntʲɪ]
boiled (~ water)	virintas	['vʲɪrʲɪntas]
to chill, cool down (vt)	atvėsinti	[atvʲeː'sʲɪntʲɪ]
to chill (vi)	vėsinti	[vʲeː'sʲɪntʲɪ]

| taste, flavour | skonis (v) | ['skoːnʲɪs] |
| aftertaste | prieskonis (v) | ['prʲiɛskonʲɪs] |

to slim down (lose weight)	laikyti dietos	[lʲʌɪ'kʲiːtʲɪ 'dʲɛtos]
diet	dieta (m)	[dʲiɛ'ta]
vitamin	vitaminas (v)	[vʲɪta'mʲɪnas]
calorie	kalorija (m)	[ka'lʲorʲɪjɛ]
vegetarian (n)	vegetaras (v)	[vʲɛgʲɛ'taːras]
vegetarian (adj)	vegetāriškas	[vʲɛgʲɛ'taːrʲɪʃkas]

fats (nutrient)	riebalai (v dgs)	[rʲiɛba'lʲʌɪ]
proteins	baltymai (v dgs)	[balʲtʲiː'mʌɪ]
carbohydrates	angliávandeniai (v dgs)	[an'glʲævandʲɛnʲɛɪ]
slice (of lemon, ham)	griežinys (v)	[grʲiɛʒɪ'nʲiːs]
piece (of cake, pie)	gabalas (v)	['gaːbalʲas]
crumb (of bread, cake, etc.)	trupinys (v)	[trʊpʲɪ'nʲiːs]

51. Cooked dishes

course, dish	patiekalas (v)	['paːtʲiɛkalʲas]
cuisine	virtuvė (m)	[vʲɪr'tʊvʲeː]
recipe	receptas (v)	[rʲɛ'tsʲɛptas]
portion	porcija (m)	['portsʲɪjɛ]

| salad | salotos (m) | [sa'lʲoːtos] |
| soup | sriuba (m) | [srʲʊ'ba] |

clear soup (broth)	sultinys (v)	[sʊlʲtʲɪ'nʲiːs]
sandwich (bread)	sumuštinis (v)	[sʊmʊʃ'tʲɪnʲɪs]
fried eggs	kiaušinienė (m)	[kʲɛʊʃʲɪ'nʲɛnʲeː]

hamburger (beefburger)	mėsainis (v)	[mʲeː'sʌɪnʲɪs]
beefsteak	bifšteksas (v)	[bʲɪfʃtʲɛksas]
side dish	garnyras (v)	[gar'nʲiːras]

spaghetti	spagečiai (v dgs)	[spa'gʲɛtʂʲɛɪ]
mash	bulvių košė (m)	['buːlʲvʲu: 'koːʃe:]
pizza	pica (m)	[pʲɪ'tsa]
porridge (oatmeal, etc.)	košė (m)	['koːʃe:]
omelette	omletas (v)	[om'lʲɛtas]

boiled (e.g. ~ beef)	virtas	['vʲɪrtas]
smoked (adj)	rūkytas	[ruː'kʲiː:tas]
fried (adj)	keptas	['kʲæptas]
dried (adj)	džiovintas	[dʒʲo'vʲɪntas]
frozen (adj)	šaldytas	['ʃalʲdʲiː:tas]
pickled (adj)	marinuotas	[marʲɪ'nʊatas]

sweet (sugary)	saldus	[salʲ'dʊs]
salty (adj)	sūrus	[suː'rʊs]
cold (adj)	šaltas	['ʃalʲtas]
hot (adj)	karštas	['karʃtas]
bitter (adj)	kartus	[kar'tʊs]
tasty (adj)	skanus	[ska'nʊs]

to cook in boiling water	virti	['vʲɪrtʲɪ]
to cook (dinner)	gaminti	[ga'mʲɪntʲɪ]
to fry (vt)	kepti	['kʲɛptʲɪ]
to heat up (food)	pašildyti	[pa'ʃɪlʲdʲiː:tʲɪ]

to salt (vt)	sūdyti	['suːdʲiː:tʲɪ]
to pepper (vt)	įberti pipirų	[iː'bʲɛrtʲɪ pʲɪ'pʲɪːru:]
to grate (vt)	tarkuoti	[tar'kʊatʲɪ]
peel (n)	luoba (m)	['lʲʊaba]
to peel (vt)	lupti bulves	['lʊptʲɪ 'bulʲvʲɛs]

52. Food

meat	mėsa (m)	[mʲe:'sa]
chicken	višta (m)	[vʲɪʃ'ta]
poussin	viščiukas (v)	[vʲɪʃ'tʂʲʊkas]
duck	antis (m)	['antʲɪs]
goose	žąsinas (v)	['ʒaːsʲɪnas]
game	žvėriena (m)	[ʒvʲe:'rʲiɛna]
turkey	kalakutiena (m)	[kalʲaku'tʲiɛna]

pork	kiauliena (m)	[kʲɛʊ'lʲiɛna]
veal	veršiena (m)	[vʲɛr'ʃiɛna]
lamb	aviena (m)	[a'vʲiɛna]
beef	jautiena (m)	['jɑʊtʲiɛna]
rabbit	triušis (v)	['trʲʊʃɪs]

sausage (bologna, etc.)	dešra (m)	[dʲɛʃ'ra]
vienna sausage (frankfurter)	dešrelė (m)	[dʲɛʃrʲælʲe:]
bacon	bekonas (v)	[bʲɛ'konas]
ham	kumpis (v)	['kʊmpʲɪs]
gammon	kumpis (v)	['kʊmpʲɪs]
pâté	paštetas (v)	[paʃ'tʲɛtas]
liver	kepenys (m dgs)	[kʲɛpe'nʲiː:s]

| mince (minced meat) | fáršas (v) | ['farʃas] |
| tongue | liežùvis (v) | [lʲiɛ'ʒuvʲɪs] |

egg	kiaušìnis (v)	[kʲɛu'ʃɪnʲɪs]
eggs	kiaušìniai (v dgs)	[kʲɛu'ʃɪnʲɛɪ]
egg white	báltymas (v)	['balʲtʲiːmas]
egg yolk	trynỹs (v)	[trʲiː'nʲiːs]

fish	žuvìs (m)	[ʒu'vʲɪs]
seafood	jū́ros gérybės (m dgs)	['juːros gʲeː'rʲiːbʲeːs]
crustaceans	vėžiãgyviai (v dgs)	[vʲeː'ʒʲægʲiːvʲɛɪ]
caviar	ìkrai (v dgs)	['ɪkrʌɪ]

crab	krãbas (v)	['kraːbas]
prawn	krevètė (m)	[krʲɛ'vʲɛtʲeː]
oyster	áustrė (m)	['austrʲe]
spiny lobster	langùstas (v)	[lʲan'gustas]
octopus	aštuonkójis (v)	[aʃtuɑŋ'koːjis]
squid	kalmãras (v)	[kalʲma:ras]

sturgeon	eršketíena (m)	[ɛrʃkʲɛ'tʲiʲɛna]
salmon	lašišà (m)	[lʲaʃɪ'ʃa]
halibut	õtas (v)	['o:tas]

cod	ménkė (m)	['mʲɛŋkʲe:]
mackerel	skùmbrė (m)	['skumbrʲe:]
tuna	tùnas (v)	['tunas]
eel	ungurỹs (v)	[ungu'rʲi:s]

trout	upétakis (v)	[u'pʲe:takʲɪs]
sardine	sardìnė (m)	[sar'dʲɪnʲe:]
pike	lydekà (m)	[lʲi:dʲɛ'ka]
herring	sìlkė (m)	['sʲɪlʲkʲe:]

bread	dúona (m)	['duɑna]
cheese	sū́ris (v)	['su:rʲɪs]
sugar	cùkrus (v)	['tsukrus]
salt	druskà (m)	[drus'ka]

rice	rỹžiai (v)	['rʲi:ʒʲɛɪ]
pasta (macaroni)	makarõnai (v dgs)	[maka'ro:nʌɪ]
noodles	lãkštiniai (v dgs)	['lʲa:kʃtʲɪnʲɛɪ]

butter	svíestas (v)	['svʲiɛstas]
vegetable oil	augalìnis aliẽjus (v)	[augalʲɪnʲɪs a'lʲɛjus]
sunflower oil	saulégrąžų aliẽjus (v)	[sau'lʲe:gra:ʒu: a'lʲɛjus]
margarine	margarìnas (v)	[marga'rʲɪnas]

| olives | alỹvuogės (m dgs) | [a'lʲi:vuɑgʲe:s] |
| olive oil | alỹvuogių aliẽjus (v) | [a'lʲi:vuɑgʲu: a'lʲɛjus] |

milk	píenas (v)	['pʲiɛnas]
condensed milk	sutírštintas píenas (v)	[su'tʲɪrʃtʲɪntas 'pʲiɛnas]
yogurt	jogùrtas (v)	[jɔ'gurtas]
soured cream	grietìnė (m)	[grʲiɛ'tʲɪnʲe:]
cream (of milk)	grietinėlė (m)	[grʲiɛtʲɪ'nʲe:lʲe:]

| mayonnaise | majonezas (v) | [majɔ'nʲɛzas] |
| buttercream | kremas (v) | ['krʲɛmas] |

groats (barley ~, etc.)	kruopos (m dgs)	['kruapos]
flour	miltai (v dgs)	['mʲɪlʲtʌɪ]
tinned food	konservai (v dgs)	[kɔn'sʲɛrvʌɪ]

cornflakes	kukurūzų dribsniai (v dgs)	[kuku'ruːzu: 'drʲɪbsnʲɛɪ]
honey	medus (v)	[mʲɛ'dus]
jam	džemas (v)	['dʒʲɛmas]
chewing gum	kramtomoji guma (m)	[kramto'mojɪ gu'ma]

53. Drinks

water	vanduo (v)	[van'dua]
drinking water	geriamas vanduo (v)	['gʲærʲæmas van'dua]
mineral water	mineralinis vanduo (v)	[mʲɪnʲɛ'raːlʲɪnʲɪs van'dua]

still (adj)	be gazo	['bʲɛ 'gaːzɔ]
carbonated (adj)	gazuotas	[ga'zuatas]
sparkling (adj)	gazuotas	[ga'zuatas]
ice	ledas (v)	['lʲædas]
with ice	su ledais	['su lʲɛ'dʌɪs]

non-alcoholic (adj)	nealkoholonis	[nʲɛalʲko'ɣolonʲɪs]
soft drink	nealkoholonis gerimas (v)	[nʲɛalʲko'ɣolonʲɪs 'gʲeːrʲɪmas]
refreshing drink	gaivusis gerimas (v)	[gʌɪ'vusʲɪs 'gʲeːrʲɪmas]
lemonade	limonadas (v)	[lʲɪmo'naːdas]

spirits	alkoholiniai gerimai (v dgs)	[alʲko'ɣolʲɪnʲɛɪ 'gʲeːrʲɪmʌɪ]
wine	vynas (v)	['vʲiːnas]
white wine	baltas vynas (v)	['balʲtas 'vʲiːnas]
red wine	raudonas vynas (v)	[rau'donas 'vʲiːnas]

liqueur	likeris (v)	['lʲɪkʲɛrʲɪs]
champagne	šampanas (v)	[ʃam'paːnas]
vermouth	vermutas (v)	['vʲɛrmutas]

whisky	viskis (v)	['vʲɪskʲɪs]
vodka	degtinė (m)	[dʲɛk'tʲɪnʲeː]
gin	džinas (v)	['dʒʲɪnas]
cognac	konjakas (v)	[kɔn'jaːkas]
rum	romas (v)	['romas]

coffee	kava (m)	[ka'va]
black coffee	juoda kava (m)	[jua'da ka'va]
white coffee	kava su pienu (m)	[ka'va 'su 'pʲɛnu]
cappuccino	kapučino kava (m)	[kapu'tʂɪnɔ ka'va]
instant coffee	tirpi kava (m)	[tʲɪr'pʲɪ ka'va]

milk	pienas (v)	['pʲɛnas]
cocktail	kokteilis (v)	[kɔk'tʲɛɪlʲɪs]
milkshake	pieniškas kokteilis (v)	['pʲɛnʲɪʃkas kok'tʲɛɪlʲɪs]
juice	sultys (m dgs)	['sulʲtʲiːs]

tomato juice	pomidórų sùltys (m dgs)	[pom'ı'doru: 'sᴜlᵗɯ:s]
orange juice	apelsìnų sùltys (m dgs)	[apʲɛlʲ'sʲɪnu: 'sᴜlᵗɯ:s]
freshly squeezed juice	šviežiaī spáustos sùltys (m dgs)	[ʃvʲɛ'ʒʲɛɪ 'spaᴜstos 'sᴜlᵗɯ:s]

beer	alùs (v)	[a'lʲᴜs]
lager	šviesùs alùs (v)	[ʃvʲɛ'sᴜs a'lʲᴜs]
bitter	tamsùs alùs (v)	[tam'sᴜs a'lʲᴜs]

tea	arbatà (m)	[arba'ta]
black tea	juodà arbatà (m)	[jᴜɑ'da arba'ta]
green tea	žalià arbatà (m)	[ʒa'lʲæ arba'ta]

54. Vegetables

| vegetables | daržóvės (m dgs) | [dar'ʒovʲe:s] |
| greens | žalumýnai (v) | [ʒalʲᴜ'mʲi:nʌɪ] |

tomato	pomidóras (v)	[pom'ı'doras]
cucumber	agùrkas (v)	[a'gᴜrkas]
carrot	morkà (m)	[mor'ka]
potato	bùlvė (m)	['bᴜlʲvʲe:]
onion	svogū̃nas (v)	[svo'gu:nas]
garlic	česnãkas (v)	[tʂʲɛs'na:kas]

cabbage	kopū̃stas (v)	[ko'pu:stas]
cauliflower	kalafióras (v)	[kalʲa'fʲoras]
Brussels sprouts	briùselio kopū̃stas (v)	['brʲᴜsʲɛlʲɔ ko'pu:stas]
broccoli	brokolių kopū̃stas (v)	['brokolʲu: ko'pu:stas]

beetroot	ruñkelis, burõkas (v)	['rᴜŋkʲɛlʲɪs], [bᴜ'ro:kas]
aubergine	baklažãnas (v)	[baklʲa'ʒa:nas]
courgette	agurõtis (v)	[agᴜ'ro:tʲɪs]

| pumpkin | rópė (m) | ['ropʲe:] |
| turnip | moliū̃gas (v) | [mo'lʲu:gas] |

parsley	petražolė (m)	[pʲɛ'tra:ʒolʲe:]
dill	krãpas (v)	['kra:pas]
lettuce	salóta (m)	[sa'lʲo:ta]
celery	saliẽras (v)	[sa'lʲɛras]

| asparagus | smìdras (v) | ['smʲɪdras] |
| spinach | špinãtas (v) | [ʃpʲɪ'na:tas] |

| pea | žìrniai (v dgs) | ['ʒʲɪrnʲɛɪ] |
| beans | pùpos (m dgs) | ['pᴜpos] |

| maize | kukurū̃zas (v) | [kᴜkᴜ'ru:zas] |
| kidney bean | pupẽlės (m dgs) | [pᴜ'pʲælʲe:s] |

sweet paper	pipìras (v)	[pʲɪ'pʲɪras]
radish	ridìkas (v)	[rʲɪ'dʲɪkas]
artichoke	artišòkas (v)	[artʲɪ'ʃokas]

55. Fruits. Nuts

fruit	vaìsius (v)	['vʌɪsʲʊs]
apple	obuolỹs (v)	[obʊɑ'lʲi:s]
pear	kriáušė (m)	['krʲæʊʃe:]
lemon	citrinà (m)	[tsʲɪtrʲɪ'na]
orange	apelsìnas (v)	[apʲɛlʲ'sʲɪnas]
strawberry (garden ~)	brãškė (m)	['bra:ʃkʲe:]

tangerine	mandarìnas (v)	[manda'rʲɪnas]
plum	slyvà (m)	[slʲi:'va]
peach	pérsikas (v)	['pʲɛrsʲɪkas]
apricot	abrikòsas (v)	[abrʲɪ'kosas]
raspberry	aviẽtė (m)	[a'vʲɛtʲe:]
pineapple	ananãsas (v)	[ana'na:sas]

banana	banãnas (v)	[ba'na:nas]
watermelon	arbūzas (v)	[ar'bu:zas]
grape	vỹnuogės (m dgs)	['vʲi:nʊɑgʲe:s]
sour cherry	vyšnià (m)	[vʲi:ʃnʲæ]
sweet cherry	trẽšnė (m)	['trʲæʃnʲe:]
melon	meliònas (v)	[mʲɛ'lʲonas]

grapefruit	greĩpfrutas (v)	['grʲɛɪpfrʊtas]
avocado	avokàdas (v)	[avo'kadas]
papaya	papája (m)	[pa'pa ja]
mango	màngo (v)	['mangɔ]
pomegranate	granãtas (v)	[gra'na:tas]

redcurrant	raudoníeji serbeñtai (v dgs)	[raʊdo'nʲɛji sʲɛr'bʲɛntʌɪ]
blackcurrant	juodíeji serbeñtai (v dgs)	[jʊɑ'dʲiɛjɪ sʲɛr'bʲɛntʌɪ]
gooseberry	agrãstas (v)	[ag'ra:stas]
bilberry	mėlỹnės (m dgs)	[mʲe:'lʲi:nʲe:s]
blackberry	gérvuogės (m dgs)	['gʲɛrvʊɑgʲe:s]

raisin	razìnos (m dgs)	[ra'zʲɪnos]
fig	fìgà (m)	[fʲɪ'ga]
date	datùlė (m)	[da'tʊlʲe:]

peanut	žẽmės riešutaĩ (v)	['ʒʲæmʲe:s rʲiɛʃʊ'tʌɪ]
almond	migdólas (v)	[mʲɪg'do:lʲas]
walnut	graĩkinis ríešutas (v)	['grʌɪkʲɪnʲɪs 'rʲiɛʃʊtas]
hazelnut	ríešutas (v)	['rʲiɛʃʊtas]
coconut	kòkoso ríešutas (v)	['kokosɔ 'rʲiɛʃʊtas]
pistachios	pistãcijos (m dgs)	[pʲɪs'ta:tsʲɪjɔs]

56. Bread. Sweets

bakers' confectionery (pastry)	konditèrijos gaminiaĩ (v)	[kɔndʲɪ'tʲɛrʲɪjos gamʲɪ'nʲɛɪ]
bread	dúona (m)	['dʊɑna]
biscuits	sausáiniai (v)	[saʊ'sʌɪnʲɛɪ]
chocolate (n)	šokolãdas (v)	[ʃoko'lʲa:das]
chocolate (as adj)	šokolãdinis	[ʃoko'lʲa:dʲɪnʲɪs]

candy (wrapped)	saldaìnis (v)	[salʲˈdʌˈɪnʲɪs]
cake (e.g. cupcake)	pyragáitis (v)	[pʲiːraˈgʌɪtʲɪs]
cake (e.g. birthday ~)	tòrtas (v)	[ˈtortas]

| pie (e.g. apple ~) | pyrãgas (v) | [pʲiːˈraːgas] |
| filling (for cake, pie) | įdaras (v) | [ˈiːdaras] |

jam (whole fruit jam)	uogiẽnė (m)	[ʊɑˈgʲɛnʲeː]
marmalade	marmelãdas (v)	[marmʲɛˈlʲaːdas]
wafers	vãfliai (v dgs)	[ˈvaːflʲɛɪ]
ice-cream	ledaì (v dgs)	[lʲɛˈdʌɪ]
pudding (Christmas ~)	pùdingas (v)	[ˈpʊdʲɪngas]

57. Spices

salt	druskà (m)	[drʊsˈka]
salty (adj)	sū́rus	[suːˈrʊs]
to salt (vt)	sū́dyti	[ˈsuːdʲiːtʲɪ]

black pepper	juodíeji pipìrai (v)	[jʊɑˈdʲiɛjɪ pʲɪˈpʲɪrʌɪ]
red pepper (milled ~)	raudoníeji pipìrai (v)	[rɑʊdoˈnʲiɛjɪ pʲɪˈpʲɪrʌɪ]
mustard	garstýčios (v)	[garˈstʲiːtʂʲos]
horseradish	krienaì (v dgs)	[krʲiɛˈnʌɪ]

condiment	príeskonis (v)	[ˈprʲiɛskonʲɪs]
spice	príeskonis (v)	[ˈprʲiɛskonʲɪs]
sauce	pãdažas (v)	[ˈpaːdaʒas]
vinegar	ãctas (v)	[ˈaːtstas]

anise	anýžius (v)	[aˈnʲiːʒʊs]
basil	bazìlikas (v)	[baˈzʲɪlʲɪkas]
cloves	gvazdìkas (v)	[gvazˈdʲɪkas]
ginger	imbieras (v)	[ˈɪmbʲiɛras]
coriander	kaléndra (m)	[kaˈlʲɛndra]
cinnamon	cinamònas (v)	[tsʲɪnaˈmonas]

sesame	sezãmas (v)	[sʲɛˈzaːmas]
bay leaf	láuro lãpas (v)	[ˈlʲɑʊrɔ ˈlʲaːpas]
paprika	pãprika (m)	[ˈpaːprʲɪka]
caraway	kmýnai (v)	[ˈkmʲiːnʌɪ]
saffron	šafrãnas (v)	[ʃafˈraːnas]

PERSONAL INFORMATION. FAMILY

58. Personal information. Forms

name (first name)	vardas (v)	['vardas]
surname (last name)	pavardė (m)	[pavar'dʲeː]
date of birth	gimìmo datà (m)	[gʲɪ'mʲɪmɔ da'ta]
place of birth	gimìmo vietà (m)	[gʲɪ'mʲɪmɔ vʲiɛ'ta]
nationality	tautýbė (m)	[tɑʊ'tʲiːbʲeː]
place of residence	gyvẽnamoji vietà (m)	[gʲiːvʲæna'mojɪ vʲiɛ'ta]
country	šalìs (m)	[ʃa'lʲɪs]
profession (occupation)	profèsija (m)	[profʲɛsʲɪjɛ]
gender, sex	lýtis (m)	['lʲiːtʲɪs]
height	ū̃gis (v)	['uːgʲɪs]
weight	svõris (v)	['svoːrʲɪs]

59. Family members. Relatives

mother	mótina (m)	['motʲɪna]
father	tėvas (v)	['tʲeːvas]
son	sūnùs (v)	[suː'nʊs]
daughter	dukrà, duktė̃ (m)	[dʊk'ra], [dʊk'tʲeː]
younger daughter	jaunesnióji duktė̃ (m)	[jɛʊnes'nʲoːjɪ dʊk'tʲeː]
younger son	jaunesnỹsis sūnùs (v)	[jɛʊnʲɛs'nʲiːsʲɪs suː'nʊs]
eldest daughter	vyresnióji duktė̃ (m)	[vʲiːres'nʲoːjɪ dʊk'tʲeː]
eldest son	vyresnỹsis sūnùs (v)	[vʲiːrʲɛs'nʲiːsʲɪs suː'nʊs]
brother	brólis (v)	['brolʲɪs]
elder brother	vyresnỹsis brólis (v)	[vʲiːrʲɛs'nʲiːsʲɪs 'brolʲɪs]
younger brother	jaunesnỹsis brólis (v)	[jɛʊnʲɛs'nʲiːsʲɪs 'brolʲɪs]
sister	sesuõ (m)	[sʲɛ'sʊɑ]
elder sister	vyresnióji sesuõ (m)	[vʲiːrʲɛs'nʲoːjɪ sʲɛ'sʊɑ]
younger sister	jaunesnióji sesuõ (m)	[jɛʊnʲɛs'nʲoːjɪ sʲɛ'sʊɑ]
cousin (masc.)	pùsbrolis (v)	['pʊsbrolʲɪs]
cousin (fem.)	pùsseserė (m)	['pʊseserʲeː]
mummy	mamà (m)	[ma'ma]
dad, daddy	tė̃tis (v)	['tʲeːtʲɪs]
parents	tėvaĩ (v)	[tʲeː'vʌɪ]
child	vaĩkas (v)	['vʌɪkas]
children	vaikaĩ (v)	[vʌɪ'kʌɪ]
grandmother	senẽlė (m)	[sʲɛ'nʲælʲeː]
grandfather	senẽlis (v)	[sʲɛ'nʲælʲɪs]
grandson	anū̃kas (v)	[a'nuːkas]

granddaughter	anūkė (m)	[a'nu:kʲe:]
grandchildren	anūkai (v)	[a'nu:kʌɪ]

uncle	dėdė (v)	['dʲe:dʲe:]
aunt	teta (m)	[tʲɛ'ta]
nephew	sūnénas (v)	[su:'nʲe:nas]
niece	dukterėčia (m)	[dʊkte'rʲe:tʂʲæ]

mother-in-law (wife's mother)	úošvė (m)	['ʊɑʃvʲe:]
father-in-law (husband's father)	úošvis (v)	['ʊɑʃvʲɪs]
son-in-law (daughter's husband)	žéntas (v)	['ʒʲɛntas]
stepmother	pāmotė (m)	['pa:motʲe:]
stepfather	patévis (v)	[pa'tʲe:vʲɪs]

infant	kūdikis (v)	['ku:dʲɪkʲɪs]
baby (infant)	naujāgimis (v)	[nɑʊ'ja:gʲɪmʲɪs]
little boy, kid	vaĩkas (v)	['vʌɪkas]

wife	žmona (m)	[ʒmo'na]
husband	výras (v)	['vʲi:ras]
spouse (husband)	sutuoktìnis (v)	[sʊtʊak'tʲɪnʲɪs]
spouse (wife)	sutuoktìnė (m)	[sʊtʊak'tʲɪnʲe:]

married (masc.)	vēdęs	['vʲædʲɛ:s]
married (fem.)	ištekėjusi	[ɪʃtʲɛ'kʲe:jʊsʲɪ]
single (unmarried)	vienguñgis	[vʲɛŋ'gʊŋgʲɪs]
bachelor	vienguñgis (v)	[vʲɛŋ'gʊŋgʲɪs]
divorced (masc.)	išsiskýręs	[ɪʃsʲɪ'skʲi:rʲɛ:s]
widow	našlė (m)	[naʃ'lʲe:]
widower	našlỹs (v)	[naʃ'lʲi:s]

relative	giminaĩtis (v)	[gʲɪmʲɪ'nʌɪtʲɪs]
close relative	artimas giminaĩtis (v)	['artʲɪmas gʲɪmʲɪ'nʌɪtʲɪs]
distant relative	tólimas giminaĩtis (v)	['tolʲɪmas gʲɪmʲɪ'nʌɪtʲɪs]
relatives	gìminės (m dgs)	['gʲɪmʲɪnʲe:s]

orphan (boy or girl)	našlaĩtis (v)	[naʃ'lʲʌɪtʲɪs]
guardian (of a minor)	globėjas (v)	[glʲo'bʲe:jas]
to adopt (a boy)	įsūnyti	[i:'su:nʲi:tʲɪ]
to adopt (a girl)	įdukrinti	[i:'dʊkrʲɪntʲɪ]

60. Friends. Colleagues

friend (masc.)	draūgas (v)	['drɑʊgas]
friend (fem.)	draugė (m)	[drɑʊ'gʲe:]
friendship	draugystė (m)	[drɑʊ'gʲi:stʲe:]
to be friends	draugáuti	[drɑʊ'gɑʊtʲɪ]

pal (masc.)	pažįstamas (v)	[pa'ʒʲi:stamas]
pal (fem.)	pažįstama (m)	[paʒʲi:sta'ma]
partner	pártneris (v)	['partnʲɛrʲɪs]

chief (boss)	šefas (v)	['ʃɛfas]
superior (n)	viršininkas (v)	['vʲɪrʃʲɪnʲɪŋkas]
owner, proprietor	savininkas (v)	[savʲɪ'nʲɪŋkas]
subordinate (n)	pavaldinỹs (v)	[pavalʲdʲɪ'nʲiːs]
colleague	kolegà (v)	[kɔlʲɛ'ga]

acquaintance (person)	pažį́stamas (v)	[pa'ʒʲiːstamas]
fellow traveller	pakeleĩvis (v)	[pakʲɛ'lʲɛɪvʲɪs]
classmate	klasiõkas (v)	[klʲa'sʲoːkas]

neighbour (masc.)	kaimýnas (v)	[kʌɪ'mʲiːnas]
neighbour (fem.)	kaimýnė (m)	[kʌɪ'mʲiːnʲeː]
neighbours	kaimýnai (v)	[kʌɪ'mʲiːnʌɪ]

HUMAN BODY. MEDICINE

61. Head

head	**galvà** (m)	[galʲ'va]
face	**véidas** (v)	['vʲɛɪdas]
nose	**nósis** (m)	['nosʲɪs]
mouth	**burnà** (m)	[bʊr'na]
eye	**akìs** (m)	[a'kʲɪs]
eyes	**ãkys** (m dgs)	['a:kʲi:s]
pupil	**vyzdỹs** (v)	[vʲi:z'dʲi:s]
eyebrow	**añtakis** (v)	['antakʲɪs]
eyelash	**blakstíena** (m)	[blʲak'stʲiɛna]
eyelid	**võkas** (v)	['vo:kas]
tongue	**liežùvis** (v)	[lʲiɛ'ʒʊvʲɪs]
tooth	**dantìs** (v)	[dan'tʲɪs]
lips	**lū̃pos** (m dgs)	['lʲu:pos]
cheekbones	**skruostìkauliai** (v dgs)	[skrʊɑ'stʲɪkɑʊlʲɛɪ]
gum	**dantenõs** (m dgs)	[dantʲɛ'no:s]
palate	**gomurỹs** (v)	[gomʊ'rʲi:s]
nostrils	**šnérvės** (m dgs)	['ʃnʲærvʲe:s]
chin	**smãkras** (v)	['sma:kras]
jaw	**žandìkaulis** (v)	[ʒan'dʲɪkɑʊlʲɪs]
cheek	**skrúostas** (v)	['skrʊɑstas]
forehead	**kaktà** (m)	[kak'ta]
temple	**smilkinỹs** (v)	[smʲɪlʲkʲɪ'nʲi:s]
ear	**ausìs** (m)	[ɑʊ'sʲɪs]
back of the head	**pakáušis, sprándas** (v)	[pa'kɑʊʃɪs], ['sprandas]
neck	**kãklas** (v)	['ka:klʲas]
throat	**gerklė̃** (m)	[gʲɛrk'lʲe:]
hair	**plaukaĩ** (v dgs)	[plʲɑʊ'kʌɪ]
hairstyle	**šukúosena** (m)	[ʃʊ'kʊɑsʲɛna]
haircut	**kirpìmas** (v)	[kʲɪr'pʲɪmas]
wig	**perùkas** (v)	[pʲɛ'rʊkas]
moustache	**ū̃sai** (v dgs)	['u:sʌɪ]
beard	**barzdà** (m)	[barz'da]
to have (a beard, etc.)	**nešióti**	[nʲɛ'ʃotʲɪ]
plait	**kasà** (m)	[ka'sa]
sideboards	**žándenos** (m dgs)	['ʒandʲɛnos]
red-haired (adj)	**rùdis**	['rʊdʲɪs]
grey (hair)	**žìlas**	['ʒʲɪlʲas]
bald (adj)	**plìkas**	['plʲɪkas]
bald patch	**plìkė** (m)	['plʲɪkʲe:]

| ponytail | uodegà (m) | [ʊadʲɛ'ga] |
| fringe | kìrpčiai (v dgs) | ['kʲɪrptʂʲɛɪ] |

62. Human body

| hand | pláštaka (m) | ['plʲaːʃtaka] |
| arm | rankà (m) | [raŋ'ka] |

finger	pìrštas (v)	['pʲɪrʃtas]
thumb	nykštỹs (v)	[nʲiːkʃ'tʲiːs]
little finger	mažàsis pìrštas (v)	[ma'ʒasʲɪs 'pʲɪrʃtas]
nail	nãgas (v)	['naːgas]

fist	kùmštis (v)	['kʊmʃtʲɪs]
palm	délnas (v)	['dʲɛlʲnas]
wrist	ríešas (v)	['rʲiɛʃas]
forearm	dìlbis (v)	['dʲɪlʲbʲɪs]
elbow	alkū̃nė (m)	[alʲ'kuːnʲeː]
shoulder	petìs (v)	[pʲɛ'tʲɪs]

leg	kója (m)	['koja]
foot	pėdà (m)	[pʲeː'da]
knee	kẽlias (v)	['kʲælʲæs]
calf	blauzdà (m)	[blʲɑʊz'da]
hip	šlaunìs (m)	[ʃlʲɑʊ'nʲɪs]
heel	kùlnas (v)	['kʊlʲnas]

body	kū́nas (v)	['kuːnas]
stomach	pìlvas (v)	['pʲɪlʲvas]
chest	krūtìnė (m)	[kruː'tʲɪnʲeː]
breast	krūtìs (m)	[kruː'tʲɪs]
flank	šónas (v)	['ʃonas]
back	nùgara (m)	['nʊgara]
lower back	juosmuõ (v)	[jʊas'mʊɑ]
waist	liemuõ (v)	[lʲiɛ'mʊɑ]

navel (belly button)	bámba (m)	['bamba]
buttocks	sédmenys (v dgs)	['sʲeːdmenʲiːs]
bottom	pastùrgalis, ùžpakalis (v)	[pas'tʊrgalʲɪs], ['ʊʒpakalʲɪs]

beauty spot	ãpgamas (v)	['aːpgamas]
birthmark (café au lait spot)	ãpgamas (v)	['aːpgamas]
tattoo	tatuiruõtė (m)	[tatʊi'rʊatʲeː]
scar	rándas (v)	['randas]

63. Diseases

illness	ligà (m)	[lʲɪ'ga]
to be ill	sìrgti	['sʲɪrktʲɪ]
health	sveikatà (m)	[svʲɛɪka'ta]
runny nose (coryza)	slogà (m)	[slʲo'ga]
tonsillitis	anginà (m)	[angʲɪ'na]

| cold (illness) | peršalimas (v) | ['pʲɛrʃalʲɪmas] |
| to catch a cold | peršalti | ['pʲɛrʃalʲtʲɪ] |

bronchitis	bronchìtas (v)	[bron'xʲɪtas]
pneumonia	plaučių uždegìmas (v)	['plʲɑʊt̪s̪ʲu: ʊʒdʲɛ'gʲɪmas]
flu, influenza	grìpas (v)	['grʲɪpas]

shortsighted (adj)	trumparėgis	[trʊmpa'rʲægʲɪs]
longsighted (adj)	toliarėgis	[tolʲæ'rʲægʲɪs]
strabismus (crossed eyes)	žvairùmas (v)	[ʒvʌɪ'rʊmas]
squint-eyed (adj)	žvaìras	['ʒvʌɪras]
cataract	katarakta (m)	[katarak'ta]
glaucoma	glaukoma (m)	[glʲɑʊko'ma]

stroke	insùltas (v)	[ɪn'sʊlʲtas]
heart attack	infárktas (v)	[ɪn'farktas]
myocardial infarction	miokárda infárktas (v)	[mʲɪjo'karda in'farktas]
paralysis	paralȳžius (v)	[para'lʲi:ʒʲʊs]
to paralyse (vt)	paraližúoti	[paralʲɪ'ʒʊɑtʲɪ]

allergy	alèrgija (m)	[a'lʲɛrgʲɪjɛ]
asthma	astma (m)	[ast'ma]
diabetes	diabètas (v)	[dʲɪja'bʲɛtas]

| toothache | dantų skaūsmas (v) | [dan'tu: 'skɑʊsmas] |
| caries | kāriesas (v) | ['ka:rʲɛsas] |

diarrhoea	diaréja (m)	[dʲɪjarʲeːja]
constipation	vidurių užkietéjimas (v)	[vʲɪdu'rʲu: ʊʒkʲiɛ'tʲɛjɪmas]
stomach upset	skrandžio sutrikìmas (v)	['skrandʒʲɔ sʊtrʲɪ'kʲɪmas]
food poisoning	apsinuōdijimas (v)	[apsʲɪ'nʊɑdʲɪjimas]
to get food poisoning	apsinuōdyti	[apsʲɪ'nʊɑdʲiːtʲɪ]

arthritis	artrìtas (v)	[art'rʲɪtas]
rickets	rachìtas (v)	[ra'xʲɪtas]
rheumatism	reumatìzmas (v)	[rʲɛuma'tʲɪzmas]
atherosclerosis	aterosklerozė (m)	[aterosklʲɛ'rozʲeː]

gastritis	gastrìtas (v)	[gas'trʲɪtas]
appendicitis	apendicìtas (v)	[apʲɛndʲɪ'tsʲɪtas]
cholecystitis	cholecistìtas (v)	[xolʲɛtsʲɪs'tʲɪtas]
ulcer	opa (m)	[o'pa]

measles	tymaī (v)	[tʲiː'mʌɪ]
rubella (German measles)	raudoniùkė (m)	[rɑʊdo'nʲʊkʲeː]
jaundice	geltà (m)	[gʲɛlʲ'ta]
hepatitis	hepatìtas (v)	[ɣʲɛpa'tʲɪtas]

schizophrenia	šizofrènija (m)	[ʃɪzo'frʲɛnʲɪjɛ]
rabies (hydrophobia)	pasiùtligė (m)	[pa'sʲʊtlʲɪgʲeː]
neurosis	neurozė (m)	[nʲɛʊ'rozʲeː]
concussion	smegenų sutrenkìmas (v)	[smʲɛgʲɛ'nu: sʊtrʲɛŋ'kʲɪmas]

cancer	vėžȳs (v)	[vʲeː'ʒʲiːs]
sclerosis	sklerozė (m)	[sklʲɛ'rozʲeː]
multiple sclerosis	išsėtìnė sklerozė (m)	[ɪʃsʲeː'tʲɪnʲeː sklʲɛ'rozʲeː]

alcoholism	alkoholizmas (v)	[alˈkoɣoˈlʲɪzmas]
alcoholic (n)	alokoholikas (v)	[aloko'ɣolʲɪkas]
syphilis	sifilis (v)	['sʲɪfʲɪlʲɪs]
AIDS	ŽIV (v)	['ʒɪv]

tumour	auglys (v)	[aʊgˈlʲiːs]
fever	karštligė (m)	['karʃtlʲɪgʲeː]
malaria	maliārija (m)	[maˈlʲærʲɪjɛ]
gangrene	gangrena (m)	[gangrʲɛ'na]
seasickness	jūros liga (m)	['juːros lʲɪ'ga]
epilepsy	epilepsija (m)	[ɛpʲɪ'lʲɛpsʲɪjɛ]

epidemic	epidemija (m)	[ɛpʲɪ'dʲɛmʲɪjɛ]
typhus	šiltinė (m)	['ʃɪlʲtʲɪnʲeː]
tuberculosis	tuberkuliozė (m)	[tʊberkʊ'lʲɔzʲeː]
cholera	cholera (m)	['xolʲɛra]
plague (bubonic ~)	māras (v)	['maːras]

64. Symptoms. Treatments. Part 1

symptom	simptomas (v)	[sʲɪmp'tomas]
temperature	temperatūra (m)	[tʲɛmpʲɛratu:'ra]
high temperature (fever)	aukšta temperatūra (m)	[aʊkʃ'ta tʲɛmpʲɛratu:'ra]
pulse (heartbeat)	pulsas (v)	['pʊlʲsas]

dizziness (vertigo)	galvos svaigimas (v)	[galʲ'vo:s svʌɪ'gʲɪmas]
hot (adj)	karštas	['karʃtas]
shivering	drebulys (v)	[drʲɛbʊ'lʲi:s]
pale (e.g. ~ face)	išbālęs	[ɪʃ'ba:lʲɛ:s]

cough	kosulys (v)	[kɔsʊ'lʲi:s]
to cough (vi)	kosėti	['kosʲe:tʲɪ]
to sneeze (vi)	čiaudėti	['tʃʲæʊdʲe:tʲɪ]
faint	nualpimas (v)	[nʊ'alʲpʲɪmas]
to faint (vi)	nualpti	[nʊ'alʲptʲɪ]

bruise (hématome)	mėlynė (m)	[mʲeː'lʲiːnʲeː]
bump (lump)	guzas (v)	['gʊzas]
to bang (bump)	atsitrenkti	[atsʲɪ'trʲɛŋktʲɪ]
contusion (bruise)	sumušimas (v)	[sʊmʊ'ʃɪmas]
to get a bruise	susimušti	[sʊsʲɪ'mʊʃtʲɪ]

to limp (vi)	šlubuoti	[ʃlʲʊ'bʊatʲɪ]
dislocation	išnirimas (v)	[ɪʃnʲɪ'rʲɪmas]
to dislocate (vt)	išnarinti	[ɪʃna'rʲɪntʲɪ]
fracture	lūžis (v)	['lʲuːʒɪs]
to have a fracture	susilaužyti	[sʊsʲɪ'lʲaʊʒʲiːtʲɪ]

cut (e.g. paper ~)	įpjovimas (v)	[iːpjɔ'vʲɪːmas]
to cut oneself	įsipjauti	[iːsʲɪ'pjaʊtʲɪ]
bleeding	kraujavimas (v)	[kraʊ'ja:vʲɪmas]

burn (injury)	nudegimas (v)	[nʊdʲɛ'gʲɪmas]
to get burned	nusideginti	[nʊsʲɪ'dʲæɡʲɪntʲɪ]

to prick (vt)	įdurti	[i:'dʊrtʲɪ]
to prick oneself	įsidurti	[i:sʲɪ'dʊrtʲɪ]
to injure (vt)	susižaloti	[sʊsʲɪʒa'lʲotʲɪ]
injury	sužalojimas (v)	[sʊʒa'lʲo:jɪmas]
wound	žaizda (m)	[ʒʌɪz'da]
trauma	trauma (m)	['traʊma]
to be delirious	sapalioti	[sapa'lʲotʲɪ]
to stutter (vi)	mikčioti	[mʲɪk'tʂʲotʲɪ]
sunstroke	saulės smūgis (v)	['saʊlʲe:s 'smu:gʲɪs]

65. Symptoms. Treatments. Part 2

pain, ache	skausmas (v)	['skaʊsmas]
splinter (in foot, etc.)	rakštis (m)	[rakʃ'tʲɪs]
sweat (perspiration)	prakaitas (v)	['pra:kʌɪtas]
to sweat (perspire)	prakaituoti	[prakʌɪ'tʊatʲɪ]
vomiting	pykinimas (v)	['pʲi:kʲɪnʲɪmas]
convulsions	traukuliai (v)	[traʊ'kʊlʲɛɪ]
pregnant (adj)	nėščia	[nʲe:ʃʈʂʲæ]
to be born	gimti	['gʲɪmtʲɪ]
delivery, labour	gimdymas (v)	['gʲɪmdʲi:mas]
to deliver (~ a baby)	gimdyti	[gʲɪm'dʲi:tʲɪ]
abortion	abortas (v)	[a'bortas]
breathing, respiration	kvėpavimas (v)	[kvʲe:'pa:vʲɪmas]
in-breath (inhalation)	įkvėpis (v)	['i:kvʲe:pʲɪs]
out-breath (exhalation)	iškvėpimas (v)	[ɪʃkvʲe:'pʲɪmas]
to exhale (breathe out)	iškvėpti	[ɪʃ'kvʲe:ptʲɪ]
to inhale (vi)	įkvėpti	[i:k'vʲe:ptʲɪ]
disabled person	invalidas (v)	[ɪnva'lʲɪdas]
cripple	luošys (v)	[lʲʊa'ʃʲɪ:s]
drug addict	narkomanas (v)	[narko'ma:nas]
deaf (adj)	kurčias	['kʊrtʂʲæs]
mute (adj)	nebylys	[nʲɛbʲi:'lʲi:s]
deaf mute (adj)	kurčnebylis	['kʊrtʂnʲɛbʲi:'lʲɪs]
mad, insane (adj)	pamišęs	[pa'mʲɪʃɛ:s]
madman	pamišęs (v)	[pa'mʲɪʃɛ:s]
(demented person)		
madwoman	pamišusi (m)	[pa'mʲɪʃʊsʲɪ]
to go insane	išprotėti	[ɪʃpro'tʲe:tʲɪ]
gene	genas (v)	['gʲɛnas]
immunity	imunitetas (v)	[ɪmʊnʲɪ'tʲɛtas]
hereditary (adj)	paveldimas	[pa'vʲɛlʲdʲɪmas]
congenital (adj)	įgimtas	['i:gʲɪmtas]
virus	virusas (v)	['vʲɪrʊsas]
microbe	mikrobas (v)	[mʲɪk'robas]

| bacterium | bakterija (m) | [bak'tɛrˈɪjɛ] |
| infection | infekcija (m) | [ɪnˈfʲɛktsʲɪjɛ] |

66. Symptoms. Treatments. Part 3

| hospital | ligoninė (m) | [lʲɪˈgonʲɪnʲe:] |
| patient | pacientas (v) | [paˈtsʲɪɛntas] |

diagnosis	diagnozė (m)	[dʲɪjagˈnozʲe:]
cure	gydymas (v)	[ˈgʲi:dʲi:mas]
medical treatment	gydymas (v)	[ˈgʲi:dʲi:mas]
to get treatment	gydytis	[ˈgʲi:dʲi:tʲɪs]
to treat (~ a patient)	gydyti	[ˈgʲi:dʲi:tʲɪ]
to nurse (look after)	slaugyti	[slʲɑʊˈgʲi:tʲɪ]
care (nursing ~)	slauga (m)	[slʲɑʊˈga]

operation, surgery	operacija (m)	[opʲɛˈra:tsʲɪjɛ]
to bandage (head, limb)	perrišti	[ˈpʲɛrrʲɪʃtʲɪ]
bandaging	perrišimas (v)	[ˈpʲɛrrʲɪʃɪmas]

vaccination	skiepas (v)	[ˈskʲɛpas]
to vaccinate (vt)	skiepyti	[ˈskʲɛpʲi:tʲɪ]
injection	įdūrimas (v)	[i:duˈrʲɪ:mas]
to give an injection	suleisti vaistus	[sʊˈlʲɛɪstʲɪ ˈvaɪstʊs]

attack	priepuolis (v)	[ˈprʲɪɛpʊɑlʲɪs]
amputation	amputacija (m)	[ampʊˈtaːtsʲɪjɛ]
to amputate (vt)	amputuoti	[ampʊˈtʊɑtʲɪ]
coma	koma (m)	[kɔˈma]
to be in a coma	būti komoje	[ˈbuːtʲɪ ˈkõmojɛ]
intensive care	reanimacija (m)	[rʲɛanʲɪˈmaːtsʲɪjɛ]

to recover (~ from flu)	sveikti ...	[ˈsvʲɛɪktʲɪ ...]
condition (patient's ~)	būklė (m)	[ˈbuːklʲe:]
consciousness	sąmonė (m)	[ˈsa:monʲe:]
memory (faculty)	atmintis (m)	[atmʲɪnˈtʲɪs]

to pull out (tooth)	šalinti	[ˈʃaːlʲɪntʲɪ]
filling	plomba (m)	[ˈplʲomba]
to fill (a tooth)	plombuoti	[plʲomˈbʊɑtʲɪ]

| hypnosis | hipnozė (m) | [ɣʲɪpˈnozʲe:] |
| to hypnotize (vt) | hipnotizuoti | [ɣʲɪpnotʲɪˈzʊɑtʲɪ] |

67. Medicine. Drugs. Accessories

medicine, drug	vaistas (v)	[ˈvʌɪstas]
remedy	priemonė (m)	[ˈprʲɪɛmonʲe:]
to prescribe (vt)	išrašyti	[ɪʃraˈʃɪ:tʲɪ]
prescription	receptas (v)	[rʲɛˈtsʲɛptas]
tablet, pill	tabletė (m)	[tabˈlʲɛtʲe:]
ointment	tepalas (v)	[ˈtʲæpalʲas]

ampoule	ampulė (m)	['ampʊlʲeː]
mixture, solution	mikstūra (m)	[mʲɪkstuːˈra]
syrup	sirupas (v)	['sʲɪrʊpas]
capsule	piliulė (m)	[pʲɪ'lʲʊlʲeː]
powder	milteliai (v dgs)	[mʲɪlʲ'tʲælʲɛɪ]

gauze bandage	bintas (v)	['bʲɪntas]
cotton wool	vata (m)	[va'ta]
iodine	jodas (v)	[jɔ das]

plaster	pleistras (v)	['plʲɛɪstras]
eyedropper	pipetė (m)	[pʲɪ'pʲɛtʲeː]
thermometer	termometras (v)	[tʲɛrmo'mʲɛtras]
syringe	švirkštas (v)	['ʃvʲɪrkʃtas]

wheelchair	neįgaliojo vežimėlis (v)	[nʲɛɪ:ga'lʲojɔ vʲɛ'ʒʲɪmʲeːlʲɪs]
crutches	ramentai (v dgs)	[ra'mʲɛntʌɪ]

painkiller	skausmą malšinantys vaistai (v dgs)	['skaʊsma: malʲ'ʃɪnantʲiːs 'vʌɪstʌɪ]
laxative	laisvinantys vaistai (v dgs)	['lʲʌɪsvʲɪnantʲiːs 'vʌɪstʌɪ]
spirits (ethanol)	spiritas (v)	['spʲɪrʲɪtas]
medicinal herbs	žolė (m)	[ʒo'lʲeː]
herbal (~ tea)	žolinis	[ʒo'lʲɪnʲɪs]

FLAT

68. Flat

flat	bùtas (v)	['bʊtas]
room	kambarỹs (v)	[kamba'rʲiːs]
bedroom	miegamàsis (v)	[mʲiɛga'masʲɪs]
dining room	valgomàsis (v)	[valʲgo'masʲɪs]
living room	svečių̃ kambarỹs (v)	[svʲɛ'tsʲu: kamba'rʲiːs]
study (home office)	kabinètas (v)	[kabʲɪ'nʲɛtas]

entry room	príeškambaris (v)	['prʲiɛʃkambarʲɪs]
bathroom	voniõs kambarỹs (v)	[vo'nʲoːs kamba'rʲiːs]
water closet	tualètas (v)	[tʊa'lʲɛtas]

ceiling	lùbos (m dgs)	['lʲʊbos]
floor	grĩndys (m dgs)	['grʲɪndʲiːs]
corner	kam̃pas (v)	['kampas]

69. Furniture. Interior

furniture	báldai (v)	['balʲdʌɪ]
table	stãlas (v)	['staːlʲas]
chair	kėdė̃ (m)	[kʲeː'dʲeː]
bed	lóva (m)	['lʲova]
sofa, settee	sofà (m)	[so'fa]
armchair	fòtelis (v)	['fotʲɛlʲɪs]

bookcase	spìnta (m)	['spʲɪnta]
shelf	lentýna (m)	[lʲɛn'tʲiːna]

wardrobe	drabužių̃ spìnta (m)	[dra'bʊʒʲu: 'spʲɪnta]
coat rack (wall-mounted ~)	pakabà (m)	[paka'ba]
coat stand	kabyklà (m)	[kabʲiːk'lʲa]

chest of drawers	komodà (m)	[kɔmo'da]
coffee table	žurnãlinis staliùkas (v)	[ʒʊr'naːlʲɪnʲɪs sta'lʲʊkas]

mirror	veĩdrodis (v)	['vʲɛɪdrodʲɪs]
carpet	kìlimas (v)	['kʲɪlʲɪmas]
small carpet	kilimė̃lis (v)	[kʲɪlʲɪ'mʲeːlʲɪs]

fireplace	židinỹs (v)	[ʒʲɪdʲɪ'nʲiːs]
candle	žvãkė (m)	['ʒvaːkʲeː]
candlestick	žvakìdė (m)	[ʒva'kʲɪdʲeː]

drapes	užúolaidos (m dgs)	[ʊ'ʒʊalʲʌɪdos]
wallpaper	tapètai (v)	[ta'pʲɛtʌɪ]

blinds (jalousie)	žaliuzės (m dgs)	['ʒaːlʲuzʲeːs]
table lamp	stalinė lempa (m)	[staˈlʲɪnʲeː ˈlʲɛmpa]
wall lamp (sconce)	šviestuvas (v)	[ʃvʲiɛˈstuvas]
standard lamp	toršeras (v)	[torˈʃɛras]
chandelier	sietynas (v)	[sʲiɛˈtʲiːnas]

leg (of a chair, table)	kojytė (m)	[kɔˈjiːtʲeː]
armrest	ranktūris (v)	[ˈraŋktuːrʲɪs]
back (backrest)	atlošas (v)	[ˈaːtlʲoʃas]
drawer	stalčius (v)	[ˈstalʲtʂʲus]

70. Bedding

bedclothes	patalynė (m)	[ˈpaːtalʲiːnʲeː]
pillow	pagalvė (m)	[paˈgalʲvʲeː]
pillowslip	užvalkalas (v)	[ˈuʒvalʲkalas]
duvet	užklotas (v)	[uʒˈklʲotas]
sheet	paklodė (m)	[pakˈlʲoːdʲeː]
bedspread	lovatiesė (m)	[lʲoˈvaːtʲiɛsʲeː]

71. Kitchen

kitchen	virtuvė (m)	[vʲɪrˈtuvʲeː]
gas	dujos (m dgs)	[ˈdujɔs]
gas cooker	dujinė (m)	[ˈdujinʲeː]
electric cooker	elektrinė (m)	[ɛlʲɛkˈtrʲɪnʲeː]
oven	orkaitė (m)	[ˈorkʌɪtʲeː]
microwave oven	mikrobangų krosnėlė (m)	[mʲɪkroban'gu: krosˈnʲælʲeː]

refrigerator	šaldytuvas (v)	[ʃalʲdʲiːˈtuvas]
freezer	šaldymo kamera (m)	[ˈʃalʲdʲiːmɔ ˈkaːmʲɛra]
dishwasher	indų plovimo mašina (m)	[ˈɪndu: plʲoˈvʲɪmɔ maʃɪˈna]

mincer	mėsmalė (m)	[ˈmʲeːsmalʲeː]
juicer	sulčiaspaudė (m)	[sulʲˈtʂʲæspɑudʲeː]
toaster	tosteris (v)	[ˈtostʲɛrʲɪs]
mixer	mikseris (v)	[ˈmʲɪksʲɛrʲɪs]

coffee machine	kavos aparatas (v)	[kaˈvoːs apaˈraːtas]
coffee pot	kavinukas (v)	[kavʲɪˈnukas]
coffee grinder	kavamalė (m)	[kaˈvaːmalʲeː]

kettle	arbatinukas (v)	[arbatʲɪˈnukas]
teapot	arbatinis (v)	[arbaːˈtʲɪnʲɪs]
lid	dangtelis (v)	[daŋkˈtʲælʲɪs]
tea strainer	sietelis (v)	[sʲiɛˈtʲælʲɪs]

spoon	šaukštas (v)	[ˈʃɑukʃtas]
teaspoon	arbatinis šaukštelis (v)	[arˈbaːtʲɪnʲɪs ʃɑukʃˈtʲælʲɪs]
soup spoon	valgomasis šaukštas (v)	[ˈvalʲgomasʲɪs ˈʃɑukʃtas]
fork	šakutė (m)	[ʃaˈkutʲeː]
knife	peilis (v)	[ˈpʲɛɪlʲɪs]

tableware (dishes)	iñdai (v)	['ındʌɪ]
plate (dinner ~)	lėkštė̃ (m)	[lʲeːkʃˈtʲeː]
saucer	lėkštelė̃ (m)	[lʲeːkʃˈtʲælʲeː]

shot glass	taurẽlė (m)	[tɑʊˈrʲælʲeː]
glass (tumbler)	stiklìnė (m)	[stʲɪkˈlʲɪnʲeː]
cup	puodùkas (v)	[pʊɑˈdʊkas]

sugar bowl	cùkrinė (m)	['tsʊkrʲɪnʲeː]
salt cellar	druskìnė (m)	['drʊskʲɪnʲeː]
pepper pot	pipìrinė (m)	[pʲɪˈpʲɪrʲɪnʲeː]
butter dish	svíestinė (m)	['svʲiɛstʲɪnʲeː]

stock pot (soup pot)	púodas (v)	['pʊɑdas]
frying pan (skillet)	keptùvė (m)	[kʲɛpˈtʊvʲeː]
ladle	sámtis (v)	['samtʲɪs]
colander	kiaurãsamtis (v)	[kʲɛʊˈraːsamtʲɪs]
tray (serving ~)	padėklas (v)	[paˈdʲeːklʲas]

bottle	bùtelis (v)	['bʊtʲɛlʲɪs]
jar (glass)	stiklaìnis (v)	[stʲɪkˈlʲʌɪnʲɪs]
tin (can)	skardìnė (m)	[skarˈdʲɪnʲeː]

bottle opener	atidarytùvas (v)	[atʲɪdarʲiːˈtʊvas]
tin opener	konsèrvų atidarytùvas (v)	[kɔnˈsʲɛrvu: atʲɪdarʲiːˈtʊvas]
corkscrew	kamščiãtraukis (v)	[kamʃˈtʂʲætrɑʊkʲɪs]
filter	fìltras (v)	['fʲɪlʲtras]
to filter (vt)	filtrúoti	[fʲɪlʲˈtrʊɑtʲɪ]

waste (food ~, etc.)	šiùkšlės (m dgs)	['ʃʊkʃlʲeːs]
waste bin (kitchen ~)	šiùkšlių kìbiras (v)	['ʃʊkʃlʲu: 'kʲɪbʲɪras]

72. Bathroom

bathroom	voniõs kambarỹs (v)	[voˈnʲoːs kambaˈrʲiːs]
water	vanduõ (v)	[vanˈdʊɑ]
tap	čiáupas (v)	['tʂʲæʊpas]
hot water	kárštas vanduõ (v)	['karʃtas vanˈdʊɑ]
cold water	šáltas vanduõ (v)	['ʃalʲtas vanˈdʊɑ]

toothpaste	dantų̃ pastà (m)	[danˈtuː pasˈta]
to clean one's teeth	valýti dantìs	[vaˈlʲiːtʲɪ danˈtʲɪs]
toothbrush	dantų̃ šepetėlis (v)	[danˈtuː ʃepeˈtʲeːlʲɪs]

to shave (vi)	skùstis	['skʊstʲɪs]
shaving foam	skutìmosi pùtos (m dgs)	[skʊˈtʲɪmosʲɪ 'pʊtos]
razor	skutìmosi peiliùkas (v)	[skʊˈtʲɪmosʲɪ pʲɛɪˈlʲʊkas]

to wash (one's hands, etc.)	pláuti	['plʲɑʊtʲɪ]
to have a bath	máudytis, praũstis	['mɑʊdʲiːtʲɪs], ['prɑʊstʲɪs]
shower	dùšas (v)	['dʊʃas]
to have a shower	praũstis dušè	['prɑʊstʲɪs dʊˈʃɛ]
bath	vonià (m)	[voˈnʲæ]
toilet (toilet bowl)	unitãzas (v)	[ʊnʲɪˈtaːzas]

sink (washbasin)	kriauklė (m)	[krʲɛʊkʲlʲeː]
soap	muĩlas (v)	['mʊɪlʲas]
soap dish	muĩlinė (m)	['mʊɪlʲɪnʲeː]

sponge	kempĩnė (m)	[kʲɛm'pʲɪnʲeː]
shampoo	šampūnas (v)	[ʃam'puːnas]
towel	rañkšluostis (v)	['raŋkʃlʲʊɑstʲɪs]
bathrobe	chalãtas (v)	[xa'lʲaːtas]

laundry (laundering)	skalbĩmas (v)	[skalʲ'bʲɪmas]
washing machine	skalbĩmo mašinà (m)	[skalʲ'bʲɪmɔ maʃɪ'na]
to do the laundry	skaĩbti báltinius	['skʌlʲptʲɪ 'ba lʲtʲɪnʲʊs]
washing powder	skalbĩmo miltẽliai (v dgs)	[skalʲ'bʲɪmɔ mʲɪlʲ'tʲælʲɛɪ]

73. Household appliances

TV, telly	televĩzorius (v)	[tʲɛlʲɛ'vʲɪzorʲʊs]
tape recorder	magnetofõnas (v)	[magnʲɛto'fonas]
video	video magnetofõnas (v)	[vʲɪdʲɛɔ magnʲɛto'fonas]
radio	imtùvas (v)	[ɪm'tʊvas]
player (CD, MP3, etc.)	grotùvas (v)	[gro'tʊvas]

video projector	video projèktorius (v)	['vʲɪdʲɛɔ pro'jæktorʲʊs]
home cinema	namų̃ kĩno teãtras (v)	[na'mʊ: 'kʲɪnɔ tʲɛ'a:tras]
DVD player	DVD grotùvas (v)	[dʲɪvʲɪ'dʲɪ gro'tʊvas]
amplifier	stiprintùvas (v)	[stʲɪprʲɪn'tʊvas]
video game console	žaidĩmų príedėlis (v)	[ʒʌɪ'dʲɪmu: 'prʲɪɛdʲeːlʲɪs]

video camera	videokãmera (m)	[vʲɪdʲɛo'ka:mʲɛra]
camera (photo)	fotoaparãtas (v)	[fotoapa'ra:tas]
digital camera	skaitmenĩnis fotoaparãtas (v)	[skʌɪtmʲɛ'nʲɪnʲɪs fotoapa'ra:tas]

vacuum cleaner	dùlkių siurblỹs (v)	['dʊlʲkʲu: sʲʊr'blʲi:s]
iron (e.g. steam ~)	lygintùvas (v)	[lʲi:gʲɪn'tʊvas]
ironing board	lýginimo lentà (m)	['lʲi:gʲɪnʲɪmɔ lʲɛn'ta]

telephone	telefõnas (v)	[tʲɛlʲɛ'fonas]
mobile phone	mobilùsis telefõnas (v)	[mobʲɪ'lʲʊsʲɪs tʲɛlʲɛ'fonas]
typewriter	rãšymo mašinėlė (m)	['ra:ʃɪ:mɔ maʃɪ'nʲeːlʲeː]
sewing machine	siuvĩmo mašinà (m)	[sʲʊ'vʲɪmɔ maʃɪ'na]

microphone	mikrofõnas (v)	[mʲɪkro'fonas]
headphones	ausìnės (m dgs)	[ɑu'sʲɪnʲeːs]
remote control (TV)	pùltas (v)	['pʊlʲtas]

CD, compact disc	kompãktinis dìskas (v)	[kɔm'pa:ktʲɪnʲɪs 'dʲɪskas]
cassette, tape	kasetė (m)	[ka'sʲɛtʲeː]
vinyl record	plokštẽlė (m)	[plokʃ'tʲælʲeː]

THE EARTH. WEATHER

74. Outer space

English	Lithuanian	Pronunciation
space	kosmosas (v)	['kosmosas]
space (as adj)	kosminis	['kosmʲɪnʲɪs]
outer space	kosminė erdvė (m)	['kosmʲɪnʲe: ɛrd'vʲe:]
world	visata (m)	[vʲɪsa'ta]
universe	pasaulis (v)	[pa'saʊlʲɪs]
galaxy	galaktika (m)	[ga'lʲa:ktʲɪka]
star	žvaigždė (m)	[ʒvʌɪg'ʒdʲe:]
constellation	žvaigždynas (v)	[ʒvʌɪgʒ'dʲi:nas]
planet	planeta (m)	[plʲanʲɛ'ta]
satellite	palydovas (v)	[palʲi:'do:vas]
meteorite	meteoritas (v)	[mʲɛtʲɛo'rʲɪtas]
comet	kometa (m)	[kɔmʲɛ'ta]
asteroid	asteroidas (v)	[astʲɛ'rɔɪdas]
orbit	orbita (m)	[orbʲɪ'ta]
to revolve	suktis	['sʊktʲɪs]
(~ around the Earth)		
atmosphere	atmosfera (m)	[atmosfʲɛ'ra]
the Sun	Saulė (m)	['saʊlʲe:]
solar system	Saulės sistema (m)	['saʊlʲe:s sʲɪste'ma]
solar eclipse	Saulės užtemimas (v)	['saʊlʲe:s ʊʒtʲɛ'mʲɪmas]
the Earth	Žemė (m)	['ʒʲæmʲe:]
the Moon	Mėnulis (v)	[mʲe:'nʊlʲɪs]
Mars	Marsas (v)	['marsas]
Venus	Venera (m)	[vʲɛnʲɛ'ra]
Jupiter	Jupiteris (v)	[jʊ'pʲɪtʲɛrʲɪs]
Saturn	Saturnas (v)	[sa'tʊrnas]
Mercury	Merkurijus (v)	[mʲɛr'kʊrʲɪjʊs]
Uranus	Uranas (v)	[ʊ'ra:nas]
Neptune	Neptūnas (v)	[nʲɛp'tu:nas]
Pluto	Plutonas (v)	[plʲʊ'tonas]
Milky Way	Paukščių Takas (v)	['paʊkʃʦʲu: 'ta:kas]
Great Bear (Ursa Major)	Didieji Grįžulo Ratai (v dgs)	[dʲɪ'dʲiɛjɪ 'grʲɪ:ʒʊlʲɔ 'ra:tʌɪ]
North Star	Šiaurinė žvaigždė (m)	[ʃɛʊ'rʲɪnʲe: ʒvʌɪg'ʒdʲe:]
Martian	marsietis (v)	[mar'sʲɛtʲɪs]
extraterrestrial (n)	ateivis (v)	[a'tʲɛɪvʲɪs]
alien	ateivis (v)	[a'tʲɛɪvʲɪs]

flying saucer	skraidanti lėkštė (m)	['skrʌɪdantʲɪ lʲeːkʃˈtʲeː]
spaceship	kosminis laivas (v)	['kosmʲɪnʲɪs 'lʲʌɪvas]
space station	orbitos stotis (m)	[orˈbʲɪtos stoˈtʲɪs]
blast-off	startas (v)	['startas]

engine	variklis (v)	[va'rʲɪklʲɪs]
nozzle	tūta (m)	[tuːˈta]
fuel	kuras (v)	['kuras]

| cockpit, flight deck | kabina (m) | [kabʲɪ'na] |
| aerial | antena (m) | [antʲɛ'na] |

porthole	iliuminatorius (v)	[ɪlʲumʲɪ'naːtorʲus]
solar panel	saulės baterija (m)	['saulʲeːs ba'tʲɛrʲɪjɛ]
spacesuit	skafandras (v)	[ska'fandras]

| weightlessness | nesvarumas (v) | [nʲɛsva'rumas] |
| oxygen | deguonis (v) | [dʲɛ'guanʲɪs] |

| docking (in space) | susijungimas (v) | [susʲɪjʊn'gʲɪmas] |
| to dock (vi, vt) | susijungti | [susʲɪ'jʊŋktʲɪ] |

| observatory | observatorija (m) | [obsʲɛrva'torʲɪjɛ] |
| telescope | teleskopas (v) | [tʲɛlʲɛ'skopas] |

| to observe (vt) | stebėti | [ste'bʲeːtʲɪ] |
| to explore (vt) | tyrinėti | [tʲiːrʲɪ'nʲeːtʲɪ] |

75. The Earth

the Earth	Žemė (m)	['ʒʲæmʲeː]
the globe (the Earth)	žemės rutulys (v)	['ʒʲæmʲeːs rʊtʊ'lʲiːs]
planet	planeta (m)	[plʲanʲɛ'ta]

atmosphere	atmosfera (m)	[atmosfʲɛ'ra]
geography	geografija (m)	[gʲɛo'graːfʲɪjɛ]
nature	gamta (m)	[gam'ta]

globe (table ~)	gaublys (v)	[gaub'lʲiːs]
map	žemėlapis (v)	[ʒe'mʲeːlʲapʲɪs]
atlas	atlasas (v)	['aːtlʲasas]

| Europe | Europa (m) | [ɛuro'pa] |
| Asia | azija (m) | ['aːzʲɪjɛ] |

| Africa | afrika (m) | ['aːfrʲɪka] |
| Australia | Australija (m) | [aus'traːlʲɪjɛ] |

America	Amerika (m)	[a'mʲɛrʲɪka]
North America	Šiaurės Amerika (m)	['ʃæurʲeːs a'mʲɛrʲɪka]
South America	Pietų Amerika (m)	[pʲɪɛ'tuː a'mʲɛrʲɪka]

| Antarctica | Antarktida (m) | [antarktʲɪ'da] |
| the Arctic | Arktika (m) | ['arktʲɪka] |

76. Cardinal directions

north	šiáurė (m)	[ˈʃæʊrʲe:]
to the north	į šiáurę	[i: ˈʃæʊrʲɛ:]
in the north	šiáurėje	[ˈʃæʊrʲe:je]
northern (adj)	šiaurìnis	[ʃɛʊˈrʲɪnʲɪs]
south	pietùs (v)	[pʲiɛˈtʊs]
to the south	į pietùs	[i: pʲiɛˈtʊs]
in the south	pietuosè	[pʲiɛtʊɑˈsʲɛ]
southern (adj)	pietìnis	[pʲiɛˈtʲɪnʲɪs]
west	vakaraĩ (v dgs)	[vakaˈrʌɪ]
to the west	į vākarus	[i: ˈvaːkarʊs]
in the west	vakaruosè	[vakarʊɑˈsʲɛ]
western (adj)	vakariẽtiškas	[vakaˈrʲɛtʲɪʃkas]
east	rytaĩ (v dgs)	[rʲiːˈtʌɪ]
to the east	į rýtus	[i: ˈrʲɪːtʊs]
in the east	rytuosè	[rʲiːtʊɑˈsʲɛ]
eastern (adj)	rytiẽtiškas	[rʲiːˈtʲɛtʲɪʃkas]

77. Sea. Ocean

sea	jū́ra (m)	[ˈjuːra]
ocean	vandenýnas (v)	[vandʲɛˈnʲiːnas]
gulf (bay)	įlanka (m)	[ˈiːlʲaŋka]
straits	sąsiauris (v)	[ˈsaːsʲɛʊrʲɪs]
continent (mainland)	žemýnas (v)	[ʒʲɛˈmʲiːnas]
island	sala (m)	[saˈlʲa]
peninsula	pusiãsalis (v)	[pʊˈsʲæsalʲɪs]
archipelago	archipelãgas (v)	[arxʲɪpʲɛˈlʲaːgas]
bay, cove	užutekis (v)	[ʊʒʊtʲɛkʲɪs]
harbour	úostas (v)	[ˈʊɑstas]
lagoon	lagūna (m)	[lʲaguːˈna]
cape	iškyšulỹs (v)	[ɪʃkʲiːʃʊˈlʲiːs]
atoll	atólas (v)	[aˈtolʲas]
reef	rìfas (v)	[ˈrʲɪfas]
coral	korãlas (v)	[kɔˈraːlʲas]
coral reef	korãlų rìfas (v)	[kɔˈraːlʲuː ˈrʲɪfas]
deep (adj)	gilùs	[gʲɪˈlʲʊs]
depth (deep water)	gýlis (v)	[ˈgʲiːlʲɪs]
abyss	bedugnė (m)	[bʲɛˈdʊgnʲe:]
trench (e.g. Mariana ~)	įduba (m)	[ˈiːdʊba]
current (Ocean ~)	srově (m)	[sroˈvʲe:]
to surround (bathe)	skaláuti	[skaˈlʲɑʊtʲɪ]
shore	pajūris (v)	[ˈpajuːrʲɪs]
coast	pakrántė (m)	[pakˈrantʲe:]

flow (flood tide)	antplūdis (v)	['antpl'u:d'ɪs]
ebb (ebb tide)	atoslūgis (v)	[a'tosl'u:g'ɪs]
shoal	atabradas (v)	[a'ta:bradas]
bottom (~ of the sea)	dugnas (v)	['dugnas]

wave	banga (m)	[ban'ga]
crest (~ of a wave)	bangos ketera (m)	[ban'go:s k'ɛt'ɛ'ra]
spume (sea foam)	putos (m dgs)	['putos]

storm (sea storm)	audra (m)	[aud'ra]
hurricane	uraganas (v)	[ura'ga:nas]
tsunami	cunamis (v)	[tsu'na:m'ɪs]
calm (dead ~)	štilius (v)	[ʃt'ɪ'l'us]
quiet, calm (adj)	ramus	[ra'mus]

| pole | ašigalis (v) | [a'ʃɪgal'ɪs] |
| polar (adj) | poliarinis | [po'l'ær'ɪn'ɪs] |

latitude	platuma (m)	[pl'atu'ma]
longitude	ilguma (m)	[ɪl'gu'ma]
parallel	paralelė (m)	[para'l'ɛl'e:]
equator	ekvatorius (v)	[ɛk'va:tor'us]

sky	dangus (v)	[dan'gus]
horizon	horizontas (v)	[ɣor'ɪ'zontas]
air	oras (v)	['oras]

lighthouse	švyturỹs (v)	[ʃv'i:tu'r'i:s]
to dive (vi)	nardyti	['nard'i:t'ɪ]
to sink (ab. boat)	nuskęsti	[nu'sk'ɛ:st'ɪ]
treasure	lobis (v)	['l'o:b'ɪs]

78. Seas & Oceans names

Atlantic Ocean	Atlanto vandenýnas (v)	[at'l'anto vand'ɛ'n'i:nas]
Indian Ocean	Indijos vandenýnas (v)	['ɪnd'ɪjos vand'ɛ'n'i:nas]
Pacific Ocean	Ramùsis vandenýnas (v)	[ra'mus'ɪs vand'ɛ'n'i:nas]
Arctic Ocean	Arkties vandenýnas (v)	['arkt'ɪɛs vand'ɛ'n'i:nas]

Black Sea	Juodóji jūra (m)	[jua'do:jɪ 'ju:ra]
Red Sea	Raudonóji jūra (m)	[raudo'no:jɪ 'ju:ra]
Yellow Sea	Geltonóji jūra (m)	[g'ɛl'to'no:jɪ 'ju:ra]
White Sea	Baltóji jūra (m)	[bal'to:jɪ 'ju:ra]

Caspian Sea	Kaspijos jūra (m)	['ka:sp'ɪjos 'ju:ra]
Dead Sea	Negyvóji jūra (m)	[n'ɛg'i:'vo:jɪ 'ju:ra]
Mediterranean Sea	Viduržemio jūra (m)	[v'ɪ'durʒ'ɛm'ɔ 'ju:ra]

| Aegean Sea | Egėjo jūra (m) | [ɛ'g'æjɔ 'ju:ra] |
| Adriatic Sea | adrijos jūra (m) | ['a:dr'ɪjos 'ju:ra] |

Arabian Sea	Arabijos jūra (m)	[a'rab'ɪjɔs 'ju:ra]
Sea of Japan	Japònijos jūra (m)	[ja'pon'ɪjos ju:ra]
Bering Sea	Beringo jūra (m)	['b'ɛr'ɪngɔ 'ju:ra]

South China Sea	Pietų Kinijos jūra (m)	[pʲiɛ'tu: 'kʲɪnʲɪjɔs 'juːra]
Coral Sea	Koralų jūra (m)	[kɔ'ra:lʲu: 'juːra]
Tasman Sea	Tasmānų jūra (m)	[tas'manu: 'juːra]
Caribbean Sea	Karibų jūra (m)	[ka'rʲɪbu: 'juːra]

| Barents Sea | Bārenco jūra (m) | [barʲɛntsɔ 'juːra] |
| Kara Sea | Kārsko jūra (m) | ['karskɔ 'juːra] |

North Sea	Šiáurės jūra (m)	['ʃæurʲeːs 'juːra]
Baltic Sea	Báltijos jūra (m)	['balʲtʲɪjɔs 'juːra]
Norwegian Sea	Norvėgijos jūra (m)	[nor'vʲɛgʲɪjɔs 'juːra]

79. Mountains

mountain	kálnas (v)	['kalʲnas]
mountain range	kalnų virtinė (m)	[kalʲ'nu: vʲɪrtʲɪnʲeː]
mountain ridge	kalnāgūbris (v)	[kalʲ'na:gu:brʲɪs]

summit, top	viršūnė (m)	[vʲɪr'ʃu:nʲeː]
peak	pikas (v)	['pʲɪkas]
foot (~ of the mountain)	papédė (m)	[pa'pʲeːdʲeː]
slope (mountainside)	núokalnė (m)	['nuɑkalʲnʲeː]

volcano	ugnikalnis (v)	[ug'nʲɪkalʲnʲɪs]
active volcano	veikiantis ugnikalnis (v)	['vʲɛɪkʲæntʲɪs ug'nʲɪkalʲnʲɪs]
dormant volcano	užgēsęs ugnikalnis (v)	[uʒ'gʲæsʲɛːs ug'nʲɪkalʲnʲɪs]

eruption	išsivéržimas (v)	[ɪʃsʲɪvʲɛr'ʒʲɪmas]
crater	krāteris (v)	['kra:tʲɛrʲɪs]
magma	magmā (m)	[mag'ma]
lava	lavā (m)	[lʲa'va]
molten (~ lava)	įkaĩtęs	[iː'kʌɪtʲɛːs]
canyon	kanjonas (v)	[ka'njɔ nas]
gorge	tarpùkalnė (m)	[tar'pukalʲnʲeː]
crevice	tarpēklis (m)	[tar'pʲæklʲɪs]

pass, col	kalnākelis (m)	[kalʲ'nakʲɛlʲɪs]
plateau	gulstė̃ (m)	[gulʲ'stʲeː]
cliff	uolā (m)	[uɑ'lʲa]
hill	kalvā (m)	[kalʲ'va]

glacier	ledýnas (v)	[lʲɛ'dʲiːnas]
waterfall	krioklỹs (v)	[krʲok'lʲiːs]
geyser	geĩzeris (v)	['gʲɛɪzʲɛrʲɪs]
lake	ẽžeras (v)	['ɛʒʲɛras]

plain	lygumā (m)	[lʲiːgu'ma]
landscape	peizāžas (v)	[pʲɛɪ'za:ʒas]
echo	áidas (v)	['ʌɪdas]

alpinist	alpinistas (v)	[alʲpʲɪ'nʲɪstas]
rock climber	uolakopỹs (v)	[uɑlʲako'pʲiːs]
to conquer (in climbing)	pavérgti	[pa'vʲɛrktʲɪ]
climb (an easy ~)	kopimas (v)	[kɔ'pʲɪmas]

80. Mountains names

The Alps	Álpés (m dgs)	['alʲpʲeːs]
Mont Blanc	Monblánas (v)	[mon'blʲaːnas]
The Pyrenees	Pirénai (v)	[pʲɪ'rʲeːnʌɪ]
The Carpathians	Karpãtai (v dgs)	[kar'paːtʌɪ]
The Ural Mountains	Urãlo kalnaĩ (v dgs)	[ʊ'raːlɔ kalʲ'nʌɪ]
The Caucasus Mountains	Kaukãzas (v)	[kɑʊ'kaːzas]
Mount Elbrus	Elbrùsas (v)	[ɛlʲ'brʊsas]
The Altai Mountains	Altãjus (v)	[alʲ'taːjʊs]
The Tian Shan	Tian Šãnis (v)	[tʲæn 'ʃaːnʲɪs]
The Pamirs	Pamȳras (v)	[pa'mʲiːras]
The Himalayas	Himalãjai (v dgs)	[ɣʲɪma'lʲaːjʌɪ]
Mount Everest	Everèstas (v)	[ɛvʲɛ'rʲɛstas]
The Andes	Añdai (v)	['andʌɪ]
Mount Kilimanjaro	Kilimandžãras (v)	[kʲɪlʲɪman'dʒaːras]

81. Rivers

river	ùpė (m)	['ʊpʲeː]
spring (natural source)	šaltìnis (v)	[ʃalʲ'tʲɪnʲɪs]
riverbed (river channel)	vagà (m)	[va'ga]
basin (river valley)	baseĩnas (v)	[ba'sʲɛɪnas]
to flow into ...	įtekéti į̃ ...	[iːtʲɛ'kʲeːtʲɪ iː ..]
tributary	añtplūdis (v)	['antplʲuːdʲɪs]
bank (river ~)	krañtas (v)	['krantas]
current (stream)	srově̃ (m)	[sro'vʲeː]
downstream (adv)	pasroviuĩ	[pasro'vʲʊɪ]
upstream (adv)	priẽš srõvę	['prʲɛʃ 'sroːvʲɛː]
inundation	pótvynis (v)	['potvʲiːnʲɪs]
flooding	póplūdis (v)	['poplʲuːdʲɪs]
to overflow (vi)	išsilíeti	[ɪʃsɪ'lʲiɛtʲɪ]
to flood (vt)	tvìndyti	['tvʲɪndʲiːtʲɪ]
shallow (shoal)	seklumà (m)	[sʲɛklʲʊ'ma]
rapids	sleñkstis (v)	['slʲɛŋkstʲɪs]
dam	ùžtvanka (m)	['ʊʒtvaŋka]
canal	kanãlas (v)	[ka'naːlʲas]
reservoir (artificial lake)	vandeñs saugyklà (m)	[van'dʲɛns sɑʊgʲiːk'lʲa]
sluice, lock	šliùzas (v)	['ʃlʲʊzas]
water body (pond, etc.)	vandeñs telkinȳs (v)	[van'dʲɛns tʲɛlʲkʲɪ'nʲiːs]
swamp (marshland)	pélkė (m)	['pʲɛlʲkʲeː]
bog, marsh	liū̃nas (v)	['lʲuːnas]
whirlpool	verpẽtas (v)	[vʲɛr'pʲætas]
stream (brook)	upẽlis (v)	[ʊ'pʲælʲɪs]

| drinking (ab. water) | gėriamas | ['gʲærʲæmas] |
| fresh (~ water) | gėlas | ['gʲe:lʲas] |

| ice | lėdas (v) | ['lʲædas] |
| to freeze over (ab. river, etc.) | užšalti | [ʊʒ'ʃalʲtʲɪ] |

82. Rivers names

| Seine | Sena (m) | [sʲɛ'na] |
| Loire | Luara (m) | [lʲʊa'ra] |

Thames	Temzė (m)	['tʲɛmzʲe:]
Rhine	Reinas (v)	['rʲɛɪnas]
Danube	Dunojus (v)	[dʊ'no:jʊs]

Volga	Volga (m)	['volʲga]
Don	Donas (v)	['donas]
Lena	Lena (m)	[lʲɛ'na]

Yellow River	Geltonoji upė (m)	[gʲɛlʲto'no:jɪ 'ʊpʲe:]
Yangtze	Jangdzė (m)	[jang'dzʲe:]
Mekong	Mekongas (v)	[mʲɛ'kongas]
Ganges	Gángas (v)	['gangas]

Nile River	Nilas (v)	['nʲɪlʲas]
Congo River	Kongas (v)	['kongas]
Okavango River	Okavangas (v)	[oka'va ngas]
Zambezi River	Zambezė (m)	[zam'bʲɛzʲe:]
Limpopo River	Limpopo (v)	[lʲɪmpo'po]
Misissippi River	Misisipė (m)	[mʲɪsʲɪ's'ɪpʲe:]

83. Forest

| forest, wood | miškas (v) | ['mʲɪʃkas] |
| forest (as adj) | miškinis | [mʲɪʃkʲɪnʲɪs] |

thick forest	tankumynas (v)	[taŋkʊ'mʲi:nas]
grove	giraitė (m)	[gʲɪ'rʌɪtʲe:]
forest clearing	laukas (v)	['lʲoʊkas]

| thicket | žolynas, beržynas (v) | [ʒo'lʲi:nas], [bʲɛr'ʒʲi:nas] |
| scrubland | krūmynas (v) | [kru:'mʲi:nas] |

| footpath (troddenpath) | takelis (v) | [ta'kʲælʲɪs] |
| gully | griovys (v) | [grʲo'vʲi:s] |

tree	mēdis (v)	['mʲædʲɪs]
leaf	lapas (v)	['lʲa:pas]
leaves (foliage)	lapija (m)	[lʲapʲɪ'ja]

| fall of leaves | lapų kritimas (v) | ['lʲa:pu: krʲɪ'tʲɪmas] |
| to fall (ab. leaves) | kristi | ['krʲɪstʲɪ] |

top (of the tree)	viršūnė (m)	[vʲɪrˈʃuːnʲeː]
branch	šaka (m)	[ʃaˈka]
bough	šaka (m)	[ʃaˈka]
bud (on shrub, tree)	pumpuras (v)	[ˈpʊmpʊras]
needle (of the pine tree)	spyglỹs (v)	[spʲiːgˈlʲiːs]
fir cone	kankorėžis (v)	[kaŋˈkorʲeːʒʲɪs]

tree hollow	úoksas (v)	[ˈʊɑksas]
nest	lìzdas (v)	[ˈlʲɪzdas]
burrow (animal hole)	olà (m)	[oˈlʲa]

trunk	kamíenas (v)	[kaˈmʲiɛnas]
root	šaknìs (m)	[ʃakˈnʲɪs]
bark	žievė̃ (m)	[ʒʲiɛˈvʲeː]
moss	sãmana (m)	[ˈsaːmana]

to uproot (remove trees or tree stumps)	ráuti	[ˈrɑʊtʲɪ]
to chop down	kìrsti	[ˈkʲɪrstʲɪ]
to deforest (vt)	iškìrsti	[ɪʃˈkʲɪrstʲɪ]
tree stump	kélmas (v)	[ˈkʲɛlʲmas]

campfire	láužas (v)	[ˈlʲɑʊʒas]
forest fire	gaĩsras (v)	[ˈɡʌɪsras]
to extinguish (vt)	gesìnti	[ɡʲɛˈsʲɪntʲɪ]

forest ranger	mìškininkas (v)	[ˈmʲɪʃkʲɪnʲɪŋkas]
protection	apsaugà (m)	[apsɑʊˈɡa]
to protect (~ nature)	sáugoti	[ˈsɑʊɡotʲɪ]
poacher	brakoniẽrius (v)	[brakoˈnʲɛrʲʊs]
steel trap	spą̃stai (v dgs)	[ˈspaːstʌɪ]

to pick (mushrooms)	grybáuti	[ɡrʲiːˈbɑʊtʲɪ]
to pick (berries)	uogáuti	[ʊɑˈɡɑʊtʲɪ]
to lose one's way	pasiklýsti	[pasʲɪˈklʲiːstʲɪ]

84. Natural resources

natural resources	gamtìniai ìštekliai (v dgs)	[gamˈtʲɪnʲɛɪ ˈɪʃtʲɛklʲɛɪ]
minerals	naudìngos ìškasenos (m dgs)	[nɑʊˈdʲɪngos ˈɪʃkasʲɛnos]
deposits	telkiniaĩ (v dgs)	[tʲɛlʲˈkʲɪˈnʲɛɪ]
field (e.g. oilfield)	telkinỹs (v)	[tʲɛlʲˈkʲɪˈnʲiːs]

to mine (extract)	iškàsti	[ɪʃˈkastʲɪ]
mining (extraction)	laimìkis (v)	[lʲʌɪˈmʲɪkʲɪs]
ore	rūdà (m)	[ruːˈda]
mine (e.g. for coal)	rūdýnas (v)	[ruːˈdʲiːnas]
shaft (mine ~)	šachtà (m)	[ʃaxˈta]
miner	šãchtininkas (v)	[ˈʃaːxtʲɪnʲɪŋkas]

gas (natural ~)	dùjos (m dgs)	[ˈdʊjɔs]
gas pipeline	dujótiekis (v)	[dʊˈjɔtʲɛkʲɪs]
oil (petroleum)	naftà (m)	[nafˈta]
oil pipeline	naftótiekis (v)	[nafˈtotʲɛkʲɪs]

oil well	nãftos bókštas (v)	['naːftos 'bokʃtas]
derrick (tower)	grę́žimo bókštas (v)	['grʲɛːʒʲɪmɔ 'bokʃtas]
tanker	tánklaivis (v)	['taŋklʲʌɪvʲɪs]

sand	smė̃lis (v)	['smʲeːlʲɪs]
limestone	kálkinis akmuõ (v)	['kalʲkʲɪnʲɪs akˈmʊɑ]
gravel	žvýras (v)	['ʒvʲiːras]
peat	dùrpės (m dgs)	['dʊrpʲeːs]
clay	mólis (v)	['molʲɪs]
coal	anglìs (m)	[angˈlʲɪs]

iron (ore)	geležìs (v)	[gʲɛlʲɛˈʒʲɪs]
gold	áuksas (v)	['ɑʊksas]
silver	sidãbras (v)	[sʲɪrˈdaːbras]
nickel	nìkelis (v)	['nʲɪkʲɛlʲɪs]
copper	vãris (v)	['vaːrʲɪs]

zinc	cìnkas (v)	['tsʲɪŋkas]
manganese	mangãnas (v)	[manˈgaːnas]
mercury	gývsidabris (v)	['gʲiːvsʲɪdabrʲɪs]
lead	švìnas (v)	['ʃvʲɪnas]

mineral	minerãlas (v)	[mʲɪnʲɛˈraːlʲas]
crystal	kristãlas (v)	[krʲɪsˈtaːlʲas]
marble	mármuras (v)	['marmʊras]
uranium	urãnas (v)	[ʊˈraːnas]

85. Weather

weather	óras (v)	['oras]
weather forecast	óro prognòzė (m)	['orɔ progˈnozʲeː]
temperature	temperatūrà (m)	[tʲɛmpʲɛratuːˈra]
thermometer	termomètras (v)	[tʲɛrmoˈmʲɛtras]
barometer	baromètras (v)	[baroˈmʲɛtras]

humid (adj)	drė́gnas	['drʲeːgnas]
humidity	drėgmė̃ (m)	[drʲeːgˈmʲeː]
heat (extreme ~)	kar̃štis (v)	['karʃtʲɪs]
hot (torrid)	kár̃štas	['karʃtas]
it's hot	kar̃šta	['karʃta]

| it's warm | šílta | ['ʃɪlʲta] |
| warm (moderately hot) | šíltas | ['ʃɪlʲtas] |

| it's cold | šálta | ['ʃalʲta] |
| cold (adj) | šáltas | ['ʃalʲtas] |

sun	sáulė (m)	['sɑʊlʲeː]
to shine (vi)	šviẽsti	['ʃvʲɛstʲɪ]
sunny (day)	sauléta	[sɑʊˈlʲeːta]
to come up (vi)	pakìlti	[paˈkʲɪlʲtʲɪ]
to set (vi)	léistis	['lʲɛɪstʲɪs]
cloud	debesìs (v)	[dʲɛbʲɛˈsʲɪs]
cloudy (adj)	debesúota	[dʲɛbʲɛˈsʊɑta]

| rain cloud | debesìs (v) | [dʲɛbʲɛˈsʲɪs] |
| somber (gloomy) | apsiniáukę | [apsʲɪˈnʲæʊkʲɛː] |

rain	lietùs (v)	[lʲiɛˈtʊs]
it's raining	lȳja	[ˈlʲiːja]
rainy (~ day, weather)	lietìngas	[lʲiɛˈtʲɪngas]
to drizzle (vi)	lynóti	[lʲiːˈnotʲɪ]

pouring rain	liútis (m)	[ˈlʲuːtʲɪs]
downpour	liútis (m)	[ˈlʲuːtʲɪs]
heavy (e.g. ~ rain)	stiprùs	[stʲɪpˈrʊs]
puddle	balà (m)	[baˈlʲa]
to get wet (in rain)	šlàpti	[ˈʃlʲaptʲɪ]

fog (mist)	rūkas (v)	[ˈruːkas]
foggy	miglótas	[mʲɪgˈlʲotas]
snow	sniẽgas (v)	[ˈsnʲɛgas]
it's snowing	sniñga	[ˈsnʲɪŋga]

86. Severe weather. Natural disasters

thunderstorm	perkūnija (m)	[pʲɛrˈkuːnʲɪjɛ]
lightning (~ strike)	žaĩbas (v)	[ˈʒʌɪbas]
to flash (vi)	žaibúoti	[ʒʌɪˈbʊatʲɪ]

thunder	griaustìnis (v)	[grʲɛʊsˈtʲɪnʲɪs]
to thunder (vi)	griáudėti	[ˈgrʲæʊdʲeːtʲɪ]
it's thundering	griáudėja griaustìnis	[ˈgrʲæʊdʲeːja grʲɛʊsˈtʲɪnʲɪs]

| hail | krušà (m) | [krʊˈʃa] |
| it's hailing | kriñta krušà | [ˈkrʲɪnta krʊˈʃa] |

| to flood (vt) | užlíeti | [ʊʒˈlʲiɛtʲɪ] |
| flood, inundation | pótvynis (v) | [ˈpotvʲiːnʲɪs] |

earthquake	žẽmės drebéjimas (v)	[ˈʒʲæmʲeːs dreˈbʲɛjɪmas]
tremor, shoke	smūgis (m)	[ˈsmuːgʲɪs]
epicentre	epicentras (v)	[ɛpʲɪˈtsʲɛntras]

| eruption | išsiveržìmas (v) | [ɪʃsʲɪvʲɛrˈʒʲɪmas] |
| lava | lavà (m) | [lʲaˈva] |

twister	víesulas (v)	[ˈvʲiɛsʊlʲas]
tornado	tornãdo (v)	[torˈnaːdɔ]
typhoon	taifūnas (v)	[tʌɪˈfuːnas]

hurricane	uragãnas (v)	[ʊraˈgaːnas]
storm	audrà (m)	[ɑʊdˈra]
tsunami	cunãmis (v)	[tsʊˈnaːmʲɪs]

cyclone	ciklónas (v)	[tsʲɪkˈlʲonas]
bad weather	dárgana (m)	[ˈdargana]
fire (accident)	gaĩsras (v)	[ˈgʌɪsras]
disaster	katastrofà (m)	[katastroˈfa]

meteorite	**meteorìtas** (v)	[mʲɛtʲɛoˈrʲɪtas]
avalanche	**lavinà** (m)	[lʲavʲɪˈna]
snowslide	**griūtìs** (m)	[grʲuːˈtʲɪs]
blizzard	**pūgà** (m)	[puːˈga]
snowstorm	**pūgà** (m)	[puːˈga]

FAUNA

87. Mammals. Predators

predator	plėšrūnas (v)	[plʲeːʃruːnas]
tiger	tigras (v)	['tʲɪgras]
lion	liūtas (v)	['lʲuːtas]
wolf	vilkas (v)	['vʲɪlʲkas]
fox	lapė (m)	['lʲaːpʲeː]

jaguar	jaguaras (v)	[jagʊ'aːras]
leopard	leopardas (v)	[lʲɛo'pardas]
cheetah	gepardas (v)	[gʲɛ'pardas]

black panther	pantera (m)	[pantʲɛ'ra]
puma	puma (m)	[pʊ'ma]
snow leopard	snieginis leopardas (v)	[snʲiɛ'gʲɪnʲɪs lʲɛo'pardas]
lynx	lūšis (m)	['lʲuːʃɪs]

coyote	kojotas (v)	[kɔ'jɔ tas]
jackal	šakalas (v)	[ʃa'kaːlʲas]
hyena	hiena (m)	[ɣʲiɛ'na]

88. Wild animals

| animal | gyvūnas (v) | [gʲiː'vʊːnas] |
| beast (animal) | žvėris (v) | [ʒvʲeː'rʲɪs] |

squirrel	voverė (m)	[vove'rʲeː]
hedgehog	ežys (v)	[ɛʒʲiːs]
hare	kiškis, zuikis (v)	['kʲɪʃkʲɪs], ['zʊɪkʲɪs]
rabbit	triušis (v)	['trʲʊʃɪs]

badger	barsukas (v)	[bar'sʊkas]
raccoon	meškėnas (v)	[mʲɛʃkʲeː:nas]
hamster	žiurkėnas (v)	[ʒʲʊr'kʲeː:nas]
marmot	švilpikas (v)	[ʃvʲɪlʲ'pʲɪkas]

mole	kurmis (v)	['kʊrmʲɪs]
mouse	pelė (m)	[pʲɛ'lʲeː]
rat	žiurkė (m)	['ʒʲʊrkʲeː]
bat	šikšnosparnis (v)	[ʃɪkʃ'nosparnʲɪs]

ermine	šermuonėlis (v)	[ʃermʊɑ'nʲeːlʲɪs]
sable	sabalas (v)	['sa:balʲas]
marten	kiaunė (m)	['kʲæʊnʲeː]
weasel	žebenkštis (m)	[ʒʲɛbʲɛŋkʃ'tʲɪs]
mink	audinė (m)	[ɑʊ'dʲɪnʲeː]

beaver	bėbras (v)	['bʲæbras]
otter	ūdra (m)	['uːdra]

horse	arklỹs (v)	[arkˈlʲiːs]
moose	bríedis (v)	['brʲiɛdʲɪs]
deer	élnias (v)	['ɛlʲnʲæs]
camel	kupranugāris (v)	[kupranuˈgaːrʲɪs]

bison	bizònas (v)	[bʲɪˈzonas]
wisent	stumbras (v)	['stumbras]
buffalo	buìvolas (v)	['buivolʲas]

zebra	zėbras (v)	['zʲɛbras]
antelope	antilòpė (m)	[antʲɪˈlʲopʲeː]
roe deer	stìrna (m)	['stʲɪrna]
fallow deer	daniēlius (v)	[daˈnʲɛlʲus]
chamois	gemzė (m)	['gʲɛmzʲeː]
wild boar	šérnas (v)	['ʃɛrnas]

whale	bangìnis (v)	[banˈgʲɪnʲɪs]
seal	rúonis (v)	['ruonʲɪs]
walrus	vėplỹs (v)	[vʲeːpˈlʲiːs]
fur seal	kotìkas (v)	['kotʲɪkas]
dolphin	delfìnas (v)	[dʲɛlʲˈfʲɪnas]

bear	lokỹs (v), meška (m)	[lʲoˈkʲiːs], [mʲɛʃˈka]
polar bear	baltàsis lokỹs (v)	[balʲˈtasʲɪs lʲoˈkʲiːs]
panda	pánda (m)	['panda]

monkey	beždžiõnė (m)	[bʲɛʒˈdʑʲoːnʲeː]
chimpanzee	šimpánzė (m)	[ʃɪmˈpanzʲeː]
orangutan	orangutángas (v)	[oranguˈtangas]
gorilla	gorilà (m)	[gorʲɪˈlʲa]
macaque	makakà (m)	[makaˈka]
gibbon	gibònas (v)	[gʲɪˈbonas]

elephant	dramblỹs (v)	[dramˈblʲiːs]
rhinoceros	raganòsis (v)	[ragaˈnoːsʲɪs]
giraffe	žirafà (m)	[ʒʲɪraˈfa]
hippopotamus	begemòtas (v)	[bʲɛgʲɛˈmotas]

kangaroo	kengūrà (m)	[kʲɛnˈguːˈra]
koala (bear)	koalà (m)	[kɔaˈlʲa]

mongoose	mangustà (m)	[manguˈsta]
chinchilla	šinšilà (m)	[ʃɪnʃɪˈlʲa]
skunk	skunkas (v)	['skuŋkas]
porcupine	dygliuotis (v)	[dʲiːgˈlʲuotʲɪs]

89. Domestic animals

cat	katė (m)	[kaˈtʲeː]
tomcat	katinas (v)	['kaˈtʲɪnas]
dog	šuo (v)	['ʃuɑ]

horse	arklỹs (v)	[ark'lʲiːs]
stallion (male horse)	eržilas (v)	['ɛrʒʲɪlʲas]
mare	kumělė (m)	[kʊ'mʲælʲeː]

cow	kárvė (m)	['karvʲeː]
bull	bùlius (v)	['bʊlʲʊs]
ox	jáutis (v)	['jɑʊtʲɪs]

sheep (ewe)	avìs (m)	[a'vʲɪs]
ram	ãvinas (v)	['aːvʲɪnas]
goat	ožkà (m)	[oʒ'ka]
billy goat, he-goat	ožỹs (v)	[o'ʒʲiːs]

donkey	ãsilas (v)	['aːsʲɪlʲas]
mule	mùlas (v)	['mʊlʲas]

pig	kiaŭlė (m)	['kʲɛʊlʲeː]
piglet	paršėlis (v)	[par'ʃælʲɪs]
rabbit	triùšis (v)	['trʲʊʃɪs]

hen (chicken)	vištà (m)	[vʲɪʃ'ta]
cock	gaidỹs (v)	[gʌɪ'dʲiːs]

duck	añtis (m)	['antʲɪs]
drake	añtinas (v)	['antʲɪnas]
goose	žą̃sinas (v)	['ʒaːsʲɪnas]

tom turkey, gobbler	kalakùtas (v)	[kalʲa'kʊtas]
turkey (hen)	kalakùtė (m)	[kalʲa'kʊtʲeː]

domestic animals	namìniai gyvūnai (v dgs)	[na'mʲɪnʲɛɪ gʲiːˈvuːnʌɪ]
tame (e.g. ~ hamster)	prijaukìntas	[prʲɪ'jɛʊ'kʲɪntas]
to tame (vt)	prijaukìnti	[prʲɪ'jɛʊ'kʲɪntʲɪ]
to breed (vt)	augìnti	[ɑʊ'gʲɪntʲɪ]

farm	fèrma (m)	['fʲɛrma]
poultry	namìnis paūkštis (v)	[na'mʲɪnʲɪs 'pɑʊkʃtʲɪs]
cattle	galvìjas (v)	[gal'vʲɪjɛs]
herd (cattle)	bandà (m)	[ban'da]

stable	arklìdė (m)	[ark'lʲɪdʲeː]
pigsty	kiaulìdė (m)	[kʲɛʊ'lʲɪdʲeː]
cowshed	karvìdė (m)	[kar'vʲɪdʲeː]
rabbit hutch	triušìdė (m)	[trʲʊ'ʃɪdʲeː]
hen house	vištìdė (m)	[vʲɪʃ'tʲɪdʲeː]

90. Birds

bird	paūkštis (v)	['pɑʊkʃtʲɪs]
pigeon	balañdis (v)	[ba'lʲandʲɪs]
sparrow	žvìrblis (v)	['ʒvʲɪrblʲɪs]
tit (great tit)	zýlė (m)	['zʲiːlʲeː]
magpie	šárka (m)	['ʃarka]
raven	var̃nas (v)	['varnas]

crow	várna (m)	['varna]
jackdaw	kúosa (m)	['kʊɑsa]
rook	kovàs (v)	[kɔ'vas]

duck	ántis (m)	['antʲɪs]
goose	žãsinas (v)	['ʒaːsʲɪnas]
pheasant	fazãnas (v)	[fa'zaːnas]

eagle	erẽlis (v)	[ɛ'rʲælʲɪs]
hawk	vãnagas (v)	['vaːnagas]
falcon	sãkalas (v)	['saːkalʲas]
vulture	grìfas (v)	['grʲɪfas]
condor (Andean ~)	kondòras (v)	[kɔn'doras]

swan	gulbė̃ (m)	['gʊlʲbʲeː]
crane	gérvė (m)	['gʲɛrvʲe:]
stork	gañdras (v)	['gandras]

parrot	papūgà (m)	[papuː'ga]
hummingbird	kolìbris (v)	[kɔ'lʲɪbrʲɪs]
peacock	póvas (v)	['povas]

ostrich	strùtis (v)	['strʊtʲɪs]
heron	garnỹs (v)	[gar'nʲiːs]
flamingo	flamìngas (v)	[flʲa'mʲɪngas]
pelican	pelikãnas (v)	[pʲɛlʲɪ'ka:nas]

| nightingale | lakštìngala (m) | [lʲakʃ'tʲɪŋgalʲa] |
| swallow | kregždė̃ (m) | [krʲɛgʒ'dʲe:] |

thrush	strãzdas (v)	['straːzdas]
song thrush	strãzdas giesminiñkas (v)	['straːzdas gʲiɛsmʲɪ'nʲɪŋkas]
blackbird	juodàsis strãzdas (v)	[jʊɑ'dasʲɪs s'traːzdas]

swift	čiurlỹs (v)	[tʂʲʊr'lʲiːs]
lark	vyturỹs, vieversỹs (v)	[vʲiːtʊ'rʲiːs], [vʲiɛvɛr'sʲiːs]
quail	pùtpelė (m)	['pʊtpelʲe:]

woodpecker	genỹs (v)	[gʲɛ'nʲiːs]
cuckoo	gegutė̃ (m)	[gʲɛ'gʊtʲe:]
owl	peléda (m)	[pʲɛ'lʲeːda]
eagle owl	apúokas (v)	[a'pʊɑkas]
wood grouse	kurtinỹs (v)	[kʊrtʲɪ'nʲiːs]
black grouse	tétervinas (v)	['tʲætʲɛrvʲɪnas]
partridge	kurapkà (m)	[kʊrap'ka]

starling	varnénas (v)	[var'nʲeːnas]
canary	kanarélė (m)	[kana'rʲe:lʲe:]
hazel grouse	jerubė̃ (m)	[jɛrʊ'bʲe:]

| chaffinch | kikìlis (v) | [kʲɪ'kʲɪlʲɪs] |
| bullfinch | sniẽgena (m) | ['snʲɛgʲɛna] |

seagull	žuvédra (m)	[ʒʊ'vʲe:dra]
albatross	albatròsas (v)	[alʲba't'rosas]
penguin	pingvìnas (v)	[pʲɪng'vʲɪnas]

91. Fish. Marine animals

bream	karšis (v)	['karʃɪs]
carp	kárpis (v)	['karpʲɪs]
perch	ešerys (v)	[ɛʃɛ'rʲiːs]
catfish	šãmas (v)	['ʃaːmas]
pike	lydeka (m)	[lʲiːdʲɛ'ka]

salmon	lašiša (m)	[lʲaʃɪ'ʃa]
sturgeon	erškétas (v)	[erʃ'kʲeːtas]

herring	sílkė (m)	['sʲɪlʲkʲe:]
Atlantic salmon	lašiša (m)	[lʲaʃɪ'ʃa]
mackerel	skùmbrė (m)	['skumbrʲe:]
flatfish	plẽkšnė (m)	['plʲækʃnʲe:]

zander, pike perch	starkis (v)	['starkʲɪs]
cod	ménkė (m)	['mʲɛŋkʲe:]
tuna	tùnas (v)	['tunas]
trout	upétakis (v)	[u'pʲe:takʲɪs]

eel	ungurỹs (v)	[ungu'rʲiːs]
electric ray	elektrìnė rajà (m)	[ɛlʲɛk'trʲɪnʲe: ra'ja]
moray eel	muréna (m)	[murʲɛ'na]
piranha	pirãnija (m)	[pʲɪ'raːnʲɪjɛ]

shark	ryklỹs (v)	[rʲɪk'lʲiːs]
dolphin	delfìnas (v)	[dʲɛlʲ'fɪnas]
whale	bangìnis (v)	[ban'gʲɪnʲɪs]

crab	krãbas (v)	['kraːbas]
jellyfish	medūzà (m)	[mʲɛduː'za]
octopus	aštuonkõjis (v)	[aʃtuɑŋ'koːjis]

starfish	jū́ros žvaigždė̃ (m)	['juːros ʒvʌɪgʒ'dʲe:]
sea urchin	jū́ros ežỹs (v)	['juːros ɛ'ʒʲiːs]
seahorse	jū́ros arkliùkas (v)	['juːros ark'lʲukas]

oyster	áustrė (m)	['austrʲe:]
prawn	krevètė (m)	[krʲɛ'vʲɛtʲe:]
lobster	omãras (v)	[o'maːras]
spiny lobster	langùstas (v)	[lʲan'gustas]

92. Amphibians. Reptiles

snake	gyvãtė (m)	[gʲiː'vaːtʲe:]
venomous (snake)	nuodìngas	[nuɑ'dʲɪngas]

viper	angìs (v)	[an'gʲɪs]
cobra	kobrà (m)	[kɔb'ra]
python	pitònas (v)	[pʲɪ'tonas]
boa	smauglỹs (v)	[smɑug'lʲiːs]
grass snake	žaltỹs (v)	[ʒalʲ'tʲiːs]

| rattle snake | barškuõlė (m) | [barʃ'kʊalʲe:] |
| anaconda | anakònda (m) | [ana'konda] |

lizard	dríežas (v)	['drʲiɛʒas]
iguana	iguanà (m)	[ɪgʊa'na]
monitor lizard	varãnas (v)	[va'ra:nas]
salamander	salamándra (m)	[salʲa'mandra]
chameleon	chameleònas (v)	[xamʲɛlʲɛ'ɔnas]
scorpion	skorpiònas (v)	[skorpʲɪ'ɔnas]

turtle	vėžlỹs (v)	[vʲe:ʒ'lʲi:s]
frog	varlė̃ (m)	[var'lʲe:]
toad	rùpūžė (m)	['rʊpu:ʒʲe:]
crocodile	krokodìlas (v)	[kroko'dʲɪlʲas]

93. Insects

insect	vabzdỹs (v)	[vabz'dʲi:s]
butterfly	drugẽlis (v)	[drʊ'gʲælʲɪs]
ant	skruzdėlė̃ (m)	[skrʊz'dʲælʲe:]
fly	mùsė (m)	['mʊsʲe:]
mosquito	úodas (v)	['ʊadas]
beetle	vãbalas (v)	['va:balʲas]

wasp	vapsvà (m)	[vaps'va]
bee	bìtė (m)	['bʲɪtʲe:]
bumblebee	kamãnė (m)	[ka'ma:nʲe:]
gadfly (botfly)	gylỹs (v)	[gʲi:'lʲi:s]

| spider | vóras (v) | ['voras] |
| spider's web | voratinklis (v) | [vo'ra:tʲɪŋklʲɪs] |

dragonfly	laũmžirgis (v)	['lʲaʊmʒʲɪrgʲɪs]
grasshopper	žiógas (v)	['ʒʲogas]
moth (night butterfly)	peteliškė̃ (m)	[pʲɛtʲɛ'lʲɪʃkʲe:]

cockroach	tarakõnas (v)	[tara'ko:nas]
tick	érkė (m)	[ʲærkʲe:]
flea	blusà (m)	[blʲʊ'sa]
midge	mãšalas (v)	['ma:ʃalʲas]

locust	skėrỹs (v)	[skʲe:'rʲi:s]
snail	sráigė (m)	['srʌɪgʲe:]
cricket	svirplỹs (v)	[svʲɪrp'lʲi:s]
firefly	jõnvabalis (v)	['jɔ:nvabalʲɪs]
ladybird	borùžė (m)	[bo'rʊʒʲe:]
cockchafer	grambuolỹs (v)	[grambʊa'lʲi:s]

leech	dėlė̃ (m)	[dʲe:'lʲe:]
caterpillar	vìkšras (v)	['vʲɪkʃras]
earthworm	slíekas (v)	['slʲiɛkas]
larva	kirmelė̃ (m)	[kʲɪrme'lʲe:]

FLORA

94. Trees

tree	mēdis (v)	['mʲædʲɪs]
deciduous (adj)	lapuõtis	[lʲapʊ'ɑtʲɪs]
coniferous (adj)	spygliuõtis	[spʲi:g'lʲʊo:tʲɪs]
evergreen (adj)	vìsžalis	['vʲɪsʒalʲɪs]
apple tree	obelìs (m)	[obʲɛ'lʲɪs]
pear tree	kriáušė (m)	['krʲæʊʃʲe:]
sweet cherry tree	trēšnė (m)	['trʲæʃnʲe:]
sour cherry tree	vyšnià (m)	[vʲi:ʃnʲæ]
plum tree	slyvà (m)	[slʲi:'va]
birch	béržas (v)	['bʲɛrʒas]
oak	ążuolas (v)	['a:ʒʊɑlʲas]
linden tree	líepa (m)	['lʲiɛpa]
aspen	drebulė̃ (m)	[drebʊ'lʲe:]
maple	klēvas (v)	['klʲævas]
spruce	ēglė (m)	['ʲæglʲe:]
pine	pušìs (m)	[pʊ'ʃɪs]
larch	maūmedis (v)	['mɑʊmʲɛdʲɪs]
fir tree	kẽnis (v)	['kʲe:nʲɪs]
cedar	kėdras (v)	['kʲɛdras]
poplar	túopa (m)	['tʊapa]
rowan	šermùkšnis (v)	[ʃʲɛr'mʊkʃnʲɪs]
willow	glúosnis (v)	['glʲʊɑsnʲɪs]
alder	ãlksnis (v)	['alʲksnʲɪs]
beech	bùkas (v)	['bʊkas]
elm	gúoba (m)	['gʊɑba]
ash (tree)	úosis (v)	['ʊɑsʲɪs]
chestnut	kaštõnas (v)	[kaʃ'to:nas]
magnolia	magnòlija (m)	[mag'nolʲɪjɛ]
palm tree	pálmė (m)	['palʲmʲe:]
cypress	kiparìsas (v)	[kʲɪpa'rʲɪsas]
mangrove	mañgro mēdis (v)	['maŋgrɔ 'mʲædʲɪs]
baobab	baobãbas (v)	[bao'ba:bas]
eucalyptus	eukalìptas (v)	[ɛʊka'lʲɪptas]
sequoia	sekvojà (m)	[sʲɛkvo:'jɛ]

95. Shrubs

bush	krū̃mas (v)	['kru:mas]
shrub	krūmýnas (v)	[kru:'mʲi:nas]

| grapevine | vynuogýnas (v) | [vʲiːnʊɑ'gʲiːnas] |
| vineyard | vynuogýnas (v) | [vʲiːnʊɑ'gʲiːnas] |

raspberry bush	aviẽtė (m)	[a'vʲɛtʲeː]
redcurrant bush	raudonãsis serbeñtas (v)	[rɑʊdo'nasʲɪs sʲɛr'bʲɛntas]
gooseberry bush	agrãstas (v)	[ag'raːstas]

acacia	akãcija (m)	[a'kaːtsʲɪjɛ]
barberry	raugerškis (m)	[rɑʊ'gʲɛrʃkʲɪs]
jasmine	jazmìnas (v)	[jaz'mʲɪnas]

juniper	kadagȳs (v)	[kada'gʲiːs]
rosebush	rõžių krū́mas (v)	['roːʒʲuː 'kruːmas]
dog rose	erškė́tis (v)	[erʃ'kʲeːtʲɪs]

96. Fruits. Berries

fruit	vaĩsius (v)	['vʌɪsʲʊs]
fruits	vaĩsiai (v dgs)	['vʌɪsʲɛɪ]
apple	obuolȳs (v)	[obʊɑ'lʲiːs]
pear	kriáušė (m)	['krʲæʊʃʲeː]
plum	slyvà (m)	[slʲiː'va]

strawberry (garden ~)	brãškė (m)	['braːʃkʲeː]
sour cherry	vyšnià (m)	[vʲiːʃnʲæ]
sweet cherry	trẽšnė (m)	['trʲæʃnʲeː]
grape	vȳnuogės (m dgs)	['vʲiːnʊɑgʲeːs]

raspberry	aviẽtė (m)	[a'vʲɛtʲeː]
blackcurrant	juodíeji serbeñtai (v dgs)	[jʊɑ'dʲiɛjɪ sʲɛr'bʲɛntʌɪ]
redcurrant	raudoníeji serbeñtai (v dgs)	[raʊdo'nʲɛji sʲɛr'bʲɛntʌɪ]

| gooseberry | agrãstas (v) | [ag'raːstas] |
| cranberry | spañguolė (m) | ['spaŋgʊɑlʲeː] |

orange	apelsìnas (v)	[apʲɛlʲ'sʲɪnas]
tangerine	mandarìnas (v)	[manda'rʲɪnas]
pineapple	ananãsas (v)	[ana'naːsas]

| banana | banãnas (v) | [ba'naːnas] |
| date | datùlė (m) | [da'tʊlʲeː] |

lemon	citrinà (m)	[tsʲɪtrʲɪ'na]
apricot	abrikòsas (v)	[abrʲɪ'kosas]
peach	pérsikas (v)	['pʲɛrsʲɪkas]

| kiwi | kìvis (v) | ['kʲɪvʲɪs] |
| grapefruit | greĩpfrutas (v) | ['grʲɛɪpfrʊtas] |

berry	úoga (m)	['ʊaga]
berries	úogos (m dgs)	['ʊagos]
cowberry	brùknės (m dgs)	['brʊknʲeːs]
wild strawberry	žémuogės (m dgs)	['ʒʲæmʊɑgʲeːs]
bilberry	mėlȳnės (m dgs)	[mʲeː'lʲiːnʲeːs]

97. Flowers. Plants

| flower | gėlė (m) | [gʲe:'lʲe:] |
| bouquet (of flowers) | puókštė (m) | ['puakʃtʲe:] |

rose (flower)	rõžė (m)	['ro:ʒʲe:]
tulip	tùlpė (m)	['tulʲpʲe:]
carnation	gvazdìkas (v)	[gvaz'dʲɪkas]
gladiolus	kardėlis (v)	[kar'dʲælʲɪs]

cornflower	rùgiagėlė (m)	['rugʲægʲe:lʲe:]
harebell	varpēlis (v)	[var'pʲælʲɪs]
dandelion	pienė (m)	['pʲɛnʲe:]
camomile	ramùnė (m)	[ra'munʲe:]

aloe	alijõšius (v)	[alʲɪ'jɔ:ʃus]
cactus	kãktusas (v)	['ka:ktusas]
rubber plant, ficus	fìkusas (v)	['fʲɪkusas]

lily	lelijà (m)	[lʲɛlʲɪ'ja]
geranium	pelargònija (m)	[pʲɛlʲar'gonʲɪjɛ]
hyacinth	hiacìntas (v)	[ɣʲɪja'tsʲɪntas]

mimosa	mimozà (m)	[mʲɪmo'za]
narcissus	narcìzas (v)	[nar'tsʲɪzas]
nasturtium	nastùrta (m)	[nas'turta]

orchid	orchidėja (m)	[orxʲɪ'dʲe:ja]
peony	bijūnas (v)	[bʲɪ'ju:nas]
violet	našlaitė (m)	[naʃ'lʌɪtʲe:]

pansy	darželinė našlaitė (m)	[dar'ʒʲælʲɪnʲe: naʃ'lʌɪtʲe:]
forget-me-not	neužmirštuõlė (m)	[nʲɛuʒmʲɪrʃ'tualʲe:]
daisy	saulùtė (m)	[sɑu'lʲutʲe:]

poppy	aguonà (m)	[aguɑ'na]
hemp	kanãpė (m)	[ka'na:pʲe:]
mint	mėtà (m)	[mʲe:'ta]

| lily of the valley | pakalnùtė (m) | [pakalʲ'nutʲe:] |
| snowdrop | sniēgena (m) | ['snʲɛgʲɛna] |

nettle	dilgēlė (m)	[dʲɪlʲ'gʲælʲe:]
sorrel	rūgštynė (m)	[ru:gʃ'tʲi:nʲe:]
water lily	vandeñs lelijà (m)	[van'dʲɛns lʲɛlʲɪ'ja]
fern	papártis (v)	[pa'partʲɪs]
lichen	kérpė (m)	['kʲɛrpʲe:]

conservatory (greenhouse)	oranžèrija (m)	[oran'ʒʲɛrʲɪjɛ]
lawn	gazònas (v)	[ga'zonas]
flowerbed	klòmba (m)	['klʲomba]

plant	áugalas (v)	['ɑugalʲas]
grass	žolē (m)	[ʒo'lʲe:]
blade of grass	žolēlė (m)	[ʒo'lʲælʲe:]

leaf	lãpas (v)	['lʲaːpas]
petal	žíedlapis (v)	['ʒʲiɛdlʲapʲɪs]
stem	stíebas (v)	['stʲiɛbas]
tuber	gum̃bas (v)	['gʊmbas]

| young plant (shoot) | želmuõ (v) | [ʒʲɛlʲ'mʊɑ] |
| thorn | spyglỹs (v) | [spʲiːg'lʲiːs] |

to blossom (vi)	žydéti	[ʒʲiː'dʲeːtʲɪ]
to fade, to wither	výsti	['vʲiːstʲɪ]
smell (odour)	kvãpas (v)	['kvaːpas]
to cut (flowers)	nupjáuti	[nʊ'pjɑʊtʲɪ]
to pick (a flower)	nuskìnti	[nʊ'skʲɪntʲɪ]

98. Cereals, grains

grain	grū̃das (v)	['gruːdas]
cereal crops	grūdìnės kultū̃ros (m dgs)	[gruː'dʲɪnʲeːs kʊlʲ'tuːros]
ear (of barley, etc.)	várpa (m)	['varpa]

wheat	kviečiaĩ (v dgs)	[kvʲiɛ'tʂʲɛɪ]
rye	rugiaĩ (v dgs)	[rʊ'gʲɛɪ]
oats	ãvižos (m dgs)	['aːvʲɪʒos]
millet	sóra (m)	['sora]
barley	miẽžiai (v dgs)	['mʲɛʒʲɛɪ]

maize	kukurū̃zas (v)	[kʊkʊ'ruːzas]
rice	rỹžiai (v)	['rʲiːʒʲɛɪ]
buckwheat	grìkiai (v dgs)	['grʲɪkʲɛɪ]

pea plant	žìrniai (v dgs)	['ʒʲɪrnʲɛɪ]
kidney bean	pupélės (m dgs)	[pʊ'pʲælʲeːs]
soya	sojà (m)	[soːʲjɛ]
lentil	lę̃šiai (v dgs)	['lʲɛːʃɛɪ]
beans (pulse crops)	pùpos (m dgs)	['pʊpos]

COUNTRIES OF THE WORLD

99. Countries. Part 1

Afghanistan	Afganistānas (v)	[afganʲɪ'staːnas]
Albania	Albānija (m)	[alʲ'baːnʲɪjɛ]
Argentina	Argentinà (m)	[argʲɛntʲɪ'na]
Armenia	Arménija (m)	[ar'mʲeːnʲɪjɛ]
Australia	Austrālija (m)	[ɑʊs'traːlʲɪjɛ]
Austria	Áustrija (m)	['ɑʊstrʲɪjɛ]
Azerbaijan	Azerbaidžānas (v)	[azʲɛrbʌɪ'dʒaːnas]

The Bahamas	Bahāmų salõs (m dgs)	[ba'ɣamu: 'salʲoːs]
Bangladesh	Bangladešas (v)	[banglʲa'dʲɛʃas]
Belarus	Baltarùsija (m)	[balʲta'rʊsʲɪjɛ]
Belgium	Belgija (m)	['bʲɛlˢgʲɪjɛ]
Bolivia	Bolìvija (m)	[bo'lʲɪvʲɪjɛ]
Bosnia and Herzegovina	Bosnija ir̃ Hercegovinà (m)	['bosnʲɪja ir ɣʲɛrtsʲɛgovʲɪ'na]
Brazil	Brazìlija (m)	[bra'zʲɪlʲɪjɛ]
Bulgaria	Bulgārija (m)	[bʊlʲ'gaːrʲɪjɛ]

Cambodia	Kambodžà (m)	[kambo'dʒa]
Canada	Kanadà (m)	[kana'da]
Chile	Čìlė (m)	['tʂʲɪlʲeː]
China	Kìnija (m)	['kʲɪnʲɪjɛ]
Colombia	Kolumbija (m)	[kɔ'lʲʊmbʲɪjɛ]
Croatia	Kroātija (m)	[kro'aːtʲɪjɛ]
Cuba	Kubà (m)	[kʊ'ba]

| Cyprus | Kìpras (v) | ['kʲɪpras] |
| Czech Republic | Čèkija (m) | ['tʂʲɛkʲɪjɛ] |

Denmark	Dānija (m)	['daːnʲɪjɛ]
Dominican Republic	Dominìkos Respùblika (m)	[domʲɪ'nʲɪkos rʲɛs'pʊblʲɪka]
Ecuador	Ekvadòras (v)	[ɛkva'doras]
Egypt	Egìptas (v)	[ɛ'gʲɪptas]
England	Ánglija (m)	['anglʲɪjɛ]
Estonia	Èstija (m)	['ɛstʲɪjɛ]
Finland	Suomija (m)	['sʊamʲɪjɛ]

| France | Prancūzijà (m) | [prantsu:zʲɪ'ja] |
| French Polynesia | Prancūzijos Polinèzija (m) | [prantsu:'zʲɪjos polʲɪ'nʲɛzʲɪjɛ] |

Georgia	Grùzija (m)	['grʊzʲɪjɛ]
Germany	Vokietìja (m)	[vokʲɪɛ'tʲɪja]
Ghana	Ganà (m)	[ga'na]
Great Britain	Didžiōji Britānija (m)	[dʲɪ'dʒʲoːjɪ brʲɪ'taːnʲɪjɛ]
Greece	Graìkija (m)	['grʌɪkʲɪjɛ]
Haiti	Haìtis (v)	[ɣʌ'ɪtʲɪs]
Hungary	Veñgrija (m)	['vʲɛŋgrʲɪjɛ]

100. Countries. Part 2

Iceland	Islándija (m)	[ɪs'lʲandʲɪjɛ]
India	Ìndija (m)	['ɪndʲɪjɛ]
Indonesia	Indonezijà (m)	[ɪndonʲɛzʲɪ'ja]
Iran	Irãnas (v)	[ɪ'ra:nas]
Iraq	Irãkas (v)	[ɪ'ra:kas]
Ireland	Aìrija (m)	['ʌɪrʲɪjɛ]
Israel	Izraèlis (v)	[ɪzraʲ'ɛlʲɪs]
Italy	Itãlija (m)	[ɪ'ta:lʲɪjɛ]

Jamaica	Jamáika (m)	[ja'mʌɪka]
Japan	Japònija (m)	[ja'ponʲɪjɛ]
Jordan	Jordãnija (m)	[jor'da:nʲɪjɛ]
Kazakhstan	Kazãchija (m)	[ka'za:xʲɪjɛ]
Kenya	Kènija (m)	['kʲɛnʲɪjɛ]
Kirghizia	Kirgìzija (m)	[kʲɪr'gʲɪzʲɪjɛ]
Kuwait	Kuveìtas (v)	[kʊ'vʲɛɪtas]

Laos	Laòsas (v)	[lʲa'osas]
Latvia	Làtvija (m)	['lʲa:tvʲɪjɛ]
Lebanon	Libãnas (v)	[lʲɪ'banas]
Libya	Lìbija (m)	['lʲɪbʲɪjɛ]
Liechtenstein	Lìchtenšteinas (v)	['lʲɪxtʲɛnʃtʲɛɪnas]
Lithuania	Lietuvà (m)	[lʲiɛtʊ'va]
Luxembourg	Liùksemburgas (v)	['lʲʊksʲɛmbʊrgas]

North Macedonia	Makedònija (m)	[makʲɛ'donʲɪjɛ]
Madagascar	Madagaskãras (v)	[madagas'ka:ras]
Malaysia	Maláizija (m)	[ma'lʲʌɪzʲɪjɛ]
Malta	Málta (m)	['malʲta]
Mexico	Mèksika (m)	['mʲɛksʲɪka]

Moldova, Moldavia	Moldãvija (m)	[molʲ'da:vʲɪjɛ]
Monaco	Mònakas (v)	['monakas]
Mongolia	Mongòlija (m)	[mon'golʲɪjɛ]
Montenegro	Juodkalnijà (m)	[jʊɑdkalʲnʲɪ'ja]
Morocco	Maròkas (v)	[ma'rokas]
Myanmar	Mianmãras (v)	[mʲæn'ma:ras]

Namibia	Namìbija (m)	[na'mʲɪbʲɪjɛ]
Nepal	Nepãlas (v)	[nʲɛ'pa:lʲas]
Netherlands	Nýderlandai (v dgs)	['nʲi:dʲɛrlʲandʌɪ]
New Zealand	Naujòji Zelándija (m)	[nɑʊ'jo:jɪ zʲɛ'lʲandʲɪjɛ]
North Korea	Šiáurės Koréja (m)	['ʃæʊrʲe:s ko'rʲe:ja]
Norway	Norvègija (m)	[nor'vʲɛgʲɪjɛ]

101. Countries. Part 3

Pakistan	Pakistãnas (v)	[pakʲɪ'sta:nas]
Palestine	Palestìna (m)	[palʲɛs'tʲɪna]
Panama	Panamà (m)	[pana'ma]
Paraguay	Paragvãjus (v)	[parag'va:jʊs]

Peru	Perù (v)	[pʲɛ'rʊ]
Poland	Lénkija (m)	['lʲɛŋkʲɪjɛ]
Portugal	Portugãlija (m)	[portʊ'ga:lʲɪjɛ]
Romania	Rumùnija (m)	[rʊ'mʊnʲɪjɛ]
Russia	Rùsija (m)	['rʊsʲɪjɛ]

Saudi Arabia	Saùdo Arãbija (m)	[sa'ʊdɔ a'ra:bʲɪjɛ]
Scotland	Škòtija (m)	['ʃkotʲɪjɛ]
Senegal	Senegãlas (v)	[sʲɛnʲɛ'ga:lʲas]
Serbia	Sèrbija (m)	['sʲɛrbʲɪjɛ]
Slovakia	Slovãkija (m)	[slʲo'va:kʲɪjɛ]
Slovenia	Slovénija (m)	[slʲo'vʲe:nʲɪjɛ]

South Africa	Pietų̃ ãfrikos respùblika (m)	[pʲɛ'tu: 'a:frʲɪkos rʲɛs'pʊblʲɪka]
South Korea	Pietų̃ Koréja (m)	[pʲɛ'tu: ko'rʲe:ja]
Spain	Ispãnija (m)	[ɪs'pa:nʲɪjɛ]
Suriname	Surinãmis (v)	[sʊrʲɪ'namʲɪs]
Sweden	Švèdija (m)	['ʃvʲɛdʲɪjɛ]
Switzerland	Šveicãrija (m)	[ʃvʲɛɪ'tsa:rʲɪjɛ]
Syria	Sìrija (m)	['sʲɪrʲɪjɛ]

Taiwan	Taivãnis (v)	[tʌɪ'vanʲɪs]
Tajikistan	Tadžìkija (m)	[tad'ʒɪkʲɪjɛ]
Tanzania	Tanzãnija (m)	[tan'za:nʲɪjɛ]
Tasmania	Tasmãnija (m)	[tas'ma:nʲɪjɛ]
Thailand	Tailándas (v)	[tʌɪ'lʲandas]
Tunisia	Tunìsas (v)	[tʊ'nʲɪsas]
Turkey	Tur̃kija (m)	['tʊrkʲɪjɛ]
Turkmenistan	Turkménija (m)	[tʊrk'mʲe:nʲɪjɛ]

Ukraine	Ukrainà (m)	[ʊkrʌɪ'na]
United Arab Emirates	Jungtìniai Arãbų Emiratai (v dgs)	[jʊŋk'tʲɪnʲɛɪ a'ra:bu: ɛmʲɪratʌɪ]
United States of America	Jungtìnės Amèrikos Valstìjos (m dgs)	[jʊŋk'tʲɪnʲe:s a'mʲɛrʲɪkos valʲs'tʲɪjɔs]
Uruguay	Urugvãjus (v)	[ʊrʊg'va:jʊs]
Uzbekistan	Uzbèkija (m)	[ʊz'bʲɛkʲɪjɛ]

Vatican City	Vatikãnas (v)	[vatʲɪka:nas]
Venezuela	Venesuelà (m)	[vʲɛnʲɛsʊʲɛ'lʲa]
Vietnam	Vietnãmas (v)	[vjɛt'na:mas]
Zanzibar	Zanzibãras (v)	[zanzʲɪ'ba:ras]